HD56 .S523 198

Slade, Bernard N.

Winning the productivity race

W9-DCL-228

Winning
the Productivity Race

Winning
the Productivity Race

Bernard N. Slade
Raj Mohindra

Lexington Books
D.C. Heath and Company/Lexington, Massachusetts/Toronto

Library of Congress Cataloging in Publication Data
Slade, Bernard N.
  Winning the productivity race.

  Includes index.
  1. Industrial productivity—United States.
2. Industrial management—United States.   3. Industrial
management—United States—Case studies.   I. Mohindra,
Raj.   II. Title.
HD56.S523   1985   658.5   85–40086
ISBN 0–669–10799–9 (alk. paper)

Copyright © 1985 by Bernard N. Slade and Raj Mohindra

All rights reserved. No part of this publication may be reproduced or transmitted in any form or by any means, electronic or mechanical, including photocopy, recording, or any information storage or retrieval system, without permission in writing from the publisher.

Published simultaneously in Canada
Printed in the United States of America on acid-free paper
International Standard Book Number: 0–669–10799–9
Library of Congress Catalog Card Number: 85–40086

To Margot and Nina

Contents

Figures and Tables

Figures

Tables

Acknowledgments

This book has been the result of a great deal of research and analysis and much support and assistance by many people. Much of this book has been based on the study of data that was always "there" but never properly analyzed and understood. David W. Nanek brought to bear his considerable talents to reveal basic truths. Ted Matuszewski, through his painstaking research, provided the insight into how little was really understood about the important subject of productivity.

We want to give special thanks to Professor Robert H. Hayes for giving us an early opportunity to share our ideas with his Harvard University Graduate School of Business class.

We have exchanged many of our ideas with representatives of major U.S. corporations as well as leading graduate business schools. In this regard, we would like to express our thanks to Steven C. Wheelwright, Stanford University, David A. Garvin, Harvard University, W. Burke Jackson, Brigham Young University, Willard I. Zangwill, University of Chicago, and Morris A. Cohen, University of Pennsylvania, for inviting us and providing valuable comments on our lectures.

We want to express our gratitude to Professor Roger Bohn of the Harvard University Graduate School of Business for his review of an early draft of the book and his valuable and helpful comments.

We want to thank Sherry De Matteo and Florence Graff for their invaluable assistance and patience in preparing the seemingly endless barrage of drafts and changes throughout the preparation of this book. We also wish to express our gratitude to Barbara Pierce who taught us how to write the English language and whose editing of the early portion of the book was of great assistance.

We are particularly grateful to our editor, Bruce Katz, for his invaluable critique and suggestions, which led to the final version of the book.

Raj wants to make special mention of three people who have been most important to him. He wishes to give thanks to Sri Satya Sai Baba, who was a source of great inspiration, to his father, Des Raj Mohindra, the eternal optimist who considers anything possible and has challenged the status quo with his brilliant mind, and to his mother, Pran Vati Mohindra, whose devotion and courage are exemplary.

Finally, we want to express our deepest gratitude to our wives, Margot and Nina, who supported us during periods of frustration, endured our long absences with good humor, and were our most valuable critics.

1
Introduction

This book is about productivity: the creation of goods and services to produce wealth or value. There are proven methods to dramatically increase U.S. productivity and profit. The more we produce while minimizing the increase in the energy and resources that we apply to produce it, the greater our productivity. There are many ways to cut cost and improve productivity. Machines can run faster or people can work harder; overhead can be reduced or automation of labor-intensive operations can be increased. These methods are valuable. But if productivity is the key to the United States' economic future as well as to U.S. technical leadership in the world, our society needs to take even greater strides toward economic progress than it has ever before.

Making this task difficult is the increasingly complex state of advancing technology. The postwar explosion of technology has produced computers of awesome capability, mind-boggling exploration of the solar system, and a cornucopia of exciting consumer goods. These innovations have greatly increased the complexity and sophistication of our industrial world. The potential for improving productivity is accelerating at a rapid pace, but so are the difficulties in achieving it.

This book presents some important ways to improve U.S. productivity in the face of this technological revolution. It demonstrates how we can achieve these advances using methods that have been demonstrated many times, in many places, with great success.

The United States is certainly one of the most, if not the most, innovative nations on earth. It originated the major productivity tools of our age—computers, automation, robotics, and electronics. Yet U.S. industrial productivity is at a virtual standstill,[1] while other nations that possess less industrial capital and capacity, less research and development, and far less energy and material resources, continue to increase productivity at a rapid rate. The United States needs a new perspective on the puzzling question of why, with all of its abundance of wealth and brains, it still cannot make the economic progress its people expect.

Managers need to understand what happens when potentially very productive tools are not directed properly. They also need to understand why we still use methods of performance measurement for our businesses that were valuable forty years ago but are outmoded today. These ancient techniques, designed to raise productivity, actually decrease it. How many executives know the current cost of direct labor in their business and the productivity leverage, or lack of it, in replacing that direct labor? How common is the knowledge among chief executives that conventional productivity, industrial engineering, and cost accounting techniques are of little value and are often counterproductive in achieving higher profits?

Finally, we must understand why it takes most industries in the United States two to five times as long as their counterparts in Japan to move a new product or technology from the research laboratory to the marketplace. The methods used in the past to develop and manufacture our new products no longer work, many of the skills we use are inadequate, and many of the organizational techniques that we have used so successfully in the past simply are not working well today and will be even less effective in the future.

In recent years, many observers of the U.S. economic scene have emphasized the shift from an industrial economy to a service economy and claimed that the U.S. no longer needs to worry about industrial America. They claim that the future of the United States lies in the service economy, and that other nations should be left to solve manufacturing productivity problems. We strongly disagree. The economic health of the United States demands that we compete in the world markets with products that are competitive in cost, quality, and performance. We believe that we must compete and that we can. This book explains productivity concepts and techniques that can unlock the potential for much greater productivity than experienced in the past so that we can compete. The methods used in this book are simple in concept and, with the right preparation, relatively easy to execute. Recommended here is a practical and common-sense approach to the solution of business, industrial, and manufacturing problems.

The answer to the U.S. productivity malaise does not lie in imitating the highly publicized and greatly misunderstood reasons for the economic success of other nations, nor does it lie in the use of exotic productivity tools. This book discusses two of the most important means of dramatically improving U.S. industrial productivity. First, the U.S. cycle from development to the marketplace is far too long, and far longer than some of our foreign competitors: we describe why this is so and what must be done about it. The key to shortening this cycle lies not only in how the product is developed, but in how the whole development to manufacturing and marketing process is managed. Next, we demonstrate that major productivity gains can be achieved by the proper identification of chronic constraints in U.S. manufacturing lines using some basic techniques and by allocating the necessary resources to alleviate these constraints.

The magnitude of the benefit that can be achieved by these analytical techniques depends on the efficiency that already exists in a business. Our experience indicates that a minimum productivity improvement of 10 percent can usually be attained immediately. Improvements on the order of 50 to 100 percent have been realized. Even dramatic gains far in excess of 100 percent have been achieved.

This book is divided into three sections. Part I reviews the U.S. productivity record, what U.S. industry has done to attempt to improve it, and some of the reasons for its failure. This section also discusses what U.S. top management, all the way up to the chief executive officer, must do to manage the rapid technological change that confronts us.

Part II describes specific analytical techniques that result in dramatic increases in productivity of most manufacturing lines. These techniques are applicable to practically any product, including the most complex. We show how these techniques can be applied to the design of a new production line with greatly enhanced production capability with very small increments of resources.

Part III presents seven case studies that demonstrate how major benefits can be obtained by applying the techniques described in this book. The studies were chosen to represent a wide spectrum of industries and show that these techniques can be applied with great success, even for the most complex products.

Seven principles for improving productivity should help guide all management from the CEO down:

> Accelerate the movement of products from the laboratory to the marketplace.
>
> Find the major areas of leverage and constraints in your business.
>
> Don't use piecemeal productivity improvements.
>
> Use accurate information to measure performance.
>
> Challenge your current measurement systems.
>
> Carefully target powerful productivity tools.
>
> Apply direct labor strategically.

We will discuss these principles in detail throughout the book.

This book is short. We have deliberately written it this way. We want to illustrate these methods as quickly as possible to busy business executives, economists, managers, students, and professionals and to anyone who believes that high productivity is the key to the economic future of the United States. The productivity techniques in this book are straight-forward and simple; their potential benefit, however, is enormous. The productivity leverage of using these methods in the right places can raise profits by literally hundreds of millions, even billions, of dollars. These approaches may well be the key to our economic leadership. We must not miss this opportunity.

Part I
Understanding Productivity

2
Productivity and the Chief Executive

We Must Lead or Be Left Behind

The common perception of productivity is that it is synonymous with the assembly-line worker and that the way to improve productivity is to either speed up the performance of the worker or replace him or her with an automatic tool to perform the same process. We hope that we can do something to correct this erroneous concept. Increased productivity demands far more than merely improving worker performance. It involves tools, the test apparatus, chemical and metallurgical processes, materials, the factory environment, engineers, and much more. Possibly the most important key to productivity is the management of all these resources—both the factory manager and top management, all the way up to the chief executive officer.

A spate of books in the last few years have publicized the importance of management to improved productivity. *In Search of Excellence,* by Thomas J. Peters and Robert H. Waterman, Jr., found "eight basic practices to be characteristic of successfully managed companies."[1] *The One Minute Manager,* by Ken Blanchard and Spencer Johnson, was acclaimed as "the quickest way to increase productivity, profits, job satisfaction, and personal prosperity."[2] *Megatrends,* by John Naisbitt, *Japanese Manufacturing Techniques,* by Richard Schonberger, and *Quality Is Free,* by Philip Crosby, are also notable examples of the wide publicity given to this important subject.[3] But as valuable as these books have been to the state of the art of management, far more needs to be added to the subject of productivity and how to achieve it.

The Chief Executive Officer: Today's Tactics

In order to define the problems that afflict U.S. industrial productivity, we have to look at all pieces of the puzzle. An important piece is the executive suite itself: that is where the major decisions are made, the tone of the organization set, and the strategy put in place.

A fundamental problem that seems to guide the tactics of today's chief executive was summarized in *Business Week:* "The money managers' power acts as a Damoclean sword over companies today, forcing chief executives to keep earnings on a consistently upward track, quarter by quarter, even if it means frustrating their long-range plans. And because the low value assigned to their stocks closes equity markets to most companies, managements are borrowing more to operate their businesses." As a result, "all but the largest and richest companies will be discouraged from taking risks." To cope with this environment, "more managers are turning to short-term fixes."[4]

These fixes help businesses stay alive, but they are hardly conducive to thoughtful planning and growth. Management is forced to act like a dying man in the middle of a desert, preoccupied with finding a little water to save his life, with little interest in what will happen should he ever get out of the desert alive.

What evidence supports this alarming trend? Expenditures for mergers and acquisitions are astronomical, while venture capital investments are trivial by comparison. The rate of increase in research and development and capital spending is down significantly. Buyouts are increasing. Short-term debt is increasing relative to long-term debt. As *Business Week* has pointed out, "Ultimately, that means fewer choices for consumers and investors. 'If the trend continues,' says the managing partner of a premier investment banking house, 'it means economic suicide.' "[5]

Despite this litany of gloom, the United States is still the world's industrial leader. The U.S. standard of living continues to be the envy of all nations. It continues to possess an immense reservoir of raw materials, human energy, capital, and brain power. But smugness in the face of danger signals can lead to a reversal of our fortunes. Improving industrial productivity is the major means for preventing this reversal from occurring.

Widespread recognition of and emphasis on these issues has been exhibited by the press, the government, leading graduate schools of business, and industry. All these agencies have emphasized the need for substantial increases in capital investment and research. The curricula of the leading graduate schools of business—Harvard, Stanford, Chicago, and Wharton—emphasize Japanese manufacturing techniques such as just-in-time production and total quality control. Numerous seminars across the country have been devoted to these twin strategies. U.S. corporations have invested talent and energy to adopt these seemingly magical potions as the salvation to their productivity problems. Respected publications such as the *Wall Street Journal* and *Business Week* have devoted an increasing number of articles to these Japanese manufacturing techniques.

But how beneficial are these methods, and what can they do for U.S. industry? Figure 2–1 shows just how much leverage these methods can have in solving U.S. productivity problems. This chart shows what cost and reliability improvements can be expected as a result of improving inventory and quality control techniques and what improvement can be achieved through technological innovation. The chart shows that for high technology and other growth industries, cost and quality improvements due to improved inventory and quality control methods are limited to an annual rate of 5 percent. In actual practice, even that rate of improvement is difficult to sustain. On the other hand, high technology products such as semiconductor integrated circuits, electronic packaging, magnetic disks, and fiber optics have sustained annual cost reductions as high as 25 percent as a result of technological innovations. Improvements in quality and reliability are even more dramatic; annual failure rate reductions as high as 60 percent have been sustained as a result of technological innovation.

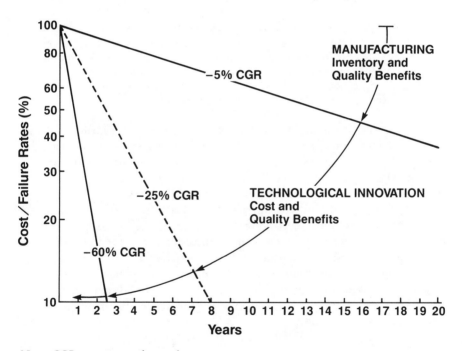

Note: CGR = compound growth rate.

Figure 2–1. Cost and Quality Benefits: Manufacturing versus Technological Innovation (High Technology and other Growth Industries)

It is clear that technological innovation is the direction the United States must take to maintain its industrial leadership. New product and process innovations will be the major means to significant improvements in industrial productivity.

Fortune featured an article on the design-to-market process which noted,

> Rapidly changing technology, quick market saturation, unexpected competition—these all make succeeding in business, particularly a high tech business, harder than ever today. Managing well, in the classical sense, isn't enough. You have to manage differently. The skills that make up the new technique—call it high-speed management—aren't easy to master. Business schools don't teach them. But learning them is becoming increasingly imperative, even in industries not commonly regarded as high tech.[6]

Robert H. Hayes and William J. Abernathy, in their article "Managing Our Way to Economic Decline," state that

> The key to long-term success—even survival—in business is what it has always been: to invest, to innovate, to lead, to create value where none existed before. Such determination, such striving to excel, requires leaders—not just controllers, market analysts, and portfolio managers. In our preoccupation with the braking systems and exterior trim, we may have neglected the drive trains of our operations.[7]

If technological innovation is the key to future success, then learning how to manage innovation will become the United States' foremost challenge. Yet today it takes much too long to translate innovations into the U.S. marketplace. To move a product from the research laboratory through the manufacturing process and into the marketplace, U.S. firms take much longer than their Japanese counterparts. Our cycle for developing, testing, refining, certifying, and entering high-volume manufacturing is simply too long. Unless major inroads are made in cutting this cycle time, we will not maintain the competitive edge we have enjoyed for so long. However, the compounded effect of even a small advantage in cycle time over foreign competition, when sustained, can have a dramatic impact on long-term economic performance. Figure 2–1 clearly demonstrates this point.

The Real versus the Publicized Japanese Strategy

Before recommending how U.S. companies should approach the problems of innovation, we want to discuss some of our opinions about

Japan. We are all bombarded by the media and the business analysts with reasons for the Japanese miracle, and almost anyone who has spent at least an hour in Tokyo poses as an authority on Japanese economics and culture. Nevertheless, the following is a capsule version of our interpretation of some of the key elements of the Japanese strategy:

Fast technological innovation. The ability of the Japanese to translate technological innovation into the marketplace faster than any other nation is the most important reason for their phenomenal productivity performance. Whether Japan can sustain this advantage will determine who will lead in the future productivity race.

Economies of scale. The combination of a protected home market that gives their manufacturing a strong base, highly leveraged operations with low interest rates for capital, the absence of antitrust laws, and a long-term strategic outlook has helped Japan produce extremely high volumes of product with the cost advantages accruing from the economies of large-scale production.

Designing quality into their products. The Japanese commitment to manufacturing quality is no secret. The conventional wisdom has taught that this high quality is due to robots, quality circles, and hard work. Without depreciating the value of these three techniques, the real Japanese quality advantages have come from superior product and process design. In a recent *Wall Street Journal* article, John Mayo, executive vice president, AT&T Bell Laboratories, states that

A new and somewhat revolutionary approach to quality control has thus been developed—"design quality," or what some call "off line" quality control. Broadly stated, off line quality control includes all quality engineering activities carried out before a product goes into full-scale production. It is not enough to come up with a product that works well when manufactured exactly according to the design specifications; the product must also be easy to manufacture and insensitive to variability on the factory floor.[8]

Proper resource allocation. Japan appears to be minimizing the resources it applies to the smokestack industries such as automobiles, machinery, appliances, garments, and so forth. It either operates these businesses on a lean-and-mean basis or uses offshore facilities to perform much of these production operations. On the other hand, Japan is applying substantial resources to the high technology industries. Japanese research and development outlays, capital investment, and manpower allocations in any given high tech industry are large and often run at levels that are two to three times higher than their U.S. competitors.

Efficient manufacturing. The efficiency of Japanese manufacturing can be measured by their high inventory turnover ratios as well as their low ratios of indirect to direct labor. Toyota operates with an inventory ratio of 70 or more, while U.S. automobile producers operate with ratios of less than 10. U.S. manufacturers generally operate with a ratio of indirect to direct workers twice or more that of Japanese companies.

Low profit margins. During the 1970s, Japanese management made increased market share its number one goal. It remains today at least number two, second only to new product development. In its effort to capture a large share of world markets, Japan has been known to operate at low profit margins and, in some cases, even at a loss.

Use of local labels/marketing in foreign countries. In yet another strategy to capture a large market share, Japanese manufacturers are linking up with manufacturers abroad. A look at recent Japanese moves in the computer industry by *Business Week* reveals that

Fujitsu has also moved aggressively to find outlets for its computers in Europe. It sold about 100 of its large computers through West Germany's Siemens last year and hopes to sign up Britain's ICL for the same number of machines this year.

Hitachi now sells its computers through Olivetti, Germany's BASF, and National Semiconductor Corp.

NEC, for example, says that it will supply Honeywell and France's Bull with at least 220 of its Large Systems 1000 machines (priced at $4 million to $5 million) over the next five years.[9]

If Japan continues to combine these strategies with its intensive concentration on product and process design, it will continue to be a formidable competitor.

Where Does the United States Go?

If the United States is going to remain in the productivity race, it must do better than it has done in the past. But to try to copy the Japanese style of management may not be only the wrong thing to do; it may actually be impossible. In fact, we don't need to copy them. The United States has the brains, the resources, and the skills to maintain its industrial leadership if it has the will to do so and the flexibility to face change.

What direction should we take to regain our productivity momentum? A key to this direction can be seen in figure 2–2. Better resource allocation, scale economics, and tangible capital form almost one-half of U.S. productivity increases. In chapter 8 we describe analytical techniques that can be applied directly to these areas. These methods have resulted in dramatic productivity increases in some businesses and can be applied to a wide range of industries. And almost one-half of U.S. productivity increases are due to technological innovations. There is little doubt that a large portion of this total is due to new technologies. Silicon technology is a prime example. The price of the simplest electronic circuit has decreased by a factor of 10,000 to 1 in the period from 1960 to 1978. The density of integrated circuits has skyrocketed from 50 transistors on a silcon chip in the 1960s to an astronomical 500,000 in the mid-1980s and continues to climb at a rapid rate.

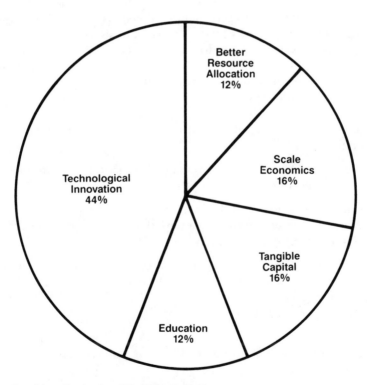

Source: Brookings Institution, Washington, D.C.

Figure 2–2. Contributors to U.S. Productivity Increases

Meeting the Productivity Challenge: The Chief Executive

If the basic foundation for corporate success is to be built by the chief executive officer, what must he do to make that foundation sound? There are four simple and obvious goals that the CEO must adopt:

Goal 1: To ensure long-term success

Goal 2: To offer leading-edge products of value to customers

Goal 3: To become bottom-line profit- (not efficiency-) oriented

Goal 4: To be the most productive

Goal 1: To Ensure Long-Term Success

Virtually every top executive in the United States will admit that the primary orientation of U.S. business is short-term success at the expense of long-term growth. Managers plan for the short term, the stockholder measures corporate progress by the yardstick of short-term performance, and executives even earn handsome incentives and bonuses based on short-term success. What can the chief executive do to meet the goal of ensuring long-term success, and what are the tests that can be applied to determine if he is doing it?

Is the CEO making substantial investments that are long-term oriented?

Does the CEO know how to manage these investments in such a way that long-term results will be achieved?

Is the CEO willing to take risks in making the necessary early investments long before there is a payoff and is he able to sell the plan to the board and stockholders?

Are the incentive plans so structured that management is motivated to plan for the long range? "What short-term CEO will take a long-term view when it lowers his own income," asks Lester Thurow. "Only a saint, and there aren't many saints."[10]

Goal 2: To Offer Leading-Edge Products of Value to Customers

Unless a business offers products of value to its customers, it will soon have neither a business nor customers. The only way a business can offer products that are of value and competitive is to get to the marketplace with a quality product sooner than its competitors. The only way it can do that is to shorten the time from invention of the product to its introduction into the marketplace. Of course, this is easier said than done. What does the CEO do to shorten the invention-to-market cycle? The answers to the following questions will indicate whether he is really doing the right things.

Do the company compensation and incentive plans reward management for making plans and taking the necessary risks and actions to accelerate the cycle?

Are sufficient technically trained people placed in influential high management positions who understand the products and technology of the company—who can make the necessary technical and business judgments needed to do a more effective and faster job of moving from the laboratory to production?

Chapter 5 will discuss what actions a company's management must take to accomplish these goals.

Goal 3: To Become Bottom-Line Profit- (Not Efficiency-) Oriented

In the face of competition, many chief executives have become efficiency-oriented. In the name of efficiency, comprehensive cost-cutting drives are organized with the objective of lowering costs. Believe it or not, these cost campaigns may actually *increase* costs. How could cutting resources increase costs, not decrease them? We devote a large part of this book to demonstrating how this can happen.

The Japanese have learned that concentrating the right resources in the right places can powerfully affect productivity. They are concentrating very high outlays for capital investment, research and development, and production engineering in the high technology and other growth industries. What may appear to be an extremely inefficient use of money may well be the nucleus of a powerful Japanese thrust for economic supremacy.

How can the chief executive know where to apply more resources to achieve productivity increases? Chapter 8 shows that major opportunities for dramatic cost and productivity improvements can result from increases in resources in the right places. It shows how to find those places, how to apply the resources, and the immense improvements that will result.

Goal 4: To Be the Most Productive

This goal is what this book is all about. Top corporate management traditionally has concentrated on financial and marketing areas. It has left the technical problems to the technical specialists. It has treated technical questions as a series of individual issues that some engineers and Ph.D.'s in isolated cubicles and laboratories, wearing T-shirts and sneakers, will solve. Top management often does not understand these issues or is not interested in them. After all, isn't that why management pays these technical people?

From the CEO's point of view, solutions to these individual technical problems are not nearly enough. The questions of technology innovation, design-to-market competitive pressures, marketing strategy, manufacturability of products, productivity of production, strategic planning, and managing the enterprise to make everything work are all highly interrelated problems in an era of high technology. There is simply no way to separate these issues into tidy compartments that lower-level management alone can attend to. The company of today and the future is a highly complex system, and management of the enterprise must have the skills, the technical training, and the insight to manage such a technically complex operation. This does not mean that every CEO must be a Ph.D. in physics. It does mean that he must understand the nature of the products and technologies that are the company's bread and butter. The CEO must be surrounded by those with technical and management skills who can assist in making the right judgments and decisions. With these skills, the CEO must be able to integrate all of the technical, marketing, financial, personnel, and production organizations so that every major action taken constitutes a total company solution rather than a series of individual and incoherent pieces. This is why the most important key to productivity is the chief executive officer.

3
Where Is the Productivity Leverage?

How to Find the Biggest Opportunities

Webster's Dictionary defines *leverage* as "the action of a lever or the mechanical advantage gained by it."[1] Loosening a large, tight bolt requires using a long wrench, not a small pair of pliers; the wrench is much more powerful and effective than the pliers. Similarly, if we want to make major inroads into the U.S. productivity problem, we need to exert powerful and effective tools. In order to understand what tools can be effective, the major contributors to productivity increases, at both the national and the industry levels, must first be identified.

The National Level

Technological innovation is the major contributor to increases in U.S. productivity. The United States has been justifiably acclaimed as the most technically innovative nation on earth. It spends more money, patents more inventions, and introduces more advanced technology than any other nation. The major production advances of the twentieth century—automation, robotics, computers, and electronics—were originated in the United States. Despite this spectacular progress, U.S. productivity performance at the national level has been poor. A major reason for this poor performance is that prolific innovation in the laboratory does not result in productivity gains until the results of innovation find their way into the marketplace. Some U.S. competitors, particularly Japan, greatly outpace the United States in moving new products and technologies from the invention state through production to the customer. In fact, Japanese cycle times from research to shipping platform are much shorter than U.S. times. Notwithstanding regulatory differences that exist and admittedly adversely affect certain U.S. industries, the Japanese have accomplished this feat with formidable teamwork among research, development, marketing, and manufacturing.

In high technology and other growth areas, aggressive cycle times can reap handsome dividends. Effectively managed they can result in annual cost and quality advantages of 50 percent and more. The time elapsed between conception of potentially valuable technical ideas and when they are actually marketed is the single most important determinant of productivity improvement. (See chapter 5 for a discussion of this subject.)

Better resource allocation, scale economics, and tangible capital expenditures are also major contributors to productivity. Much of the rest of this book (chapters 8 through 12) is devoted to an explanation of specific steps that must be taken to ensure more effective resource allocation, scale economics, and capital expenditures.

The Individual Company Level

Every company's management wants to run its operations in a lean and efficient manner. Cost-cutting campaigns are standard techniques used to eliminate waste and increase efficiency. Demands for 5 or 10 percent reductions in office and factory manpower, overhead, expense, and capital are often made. Such methods, however, may not necessarily result in higher productivity but may actually complicate the problems that they are supposed to solve. Before taking such measures, management must first understand what resources the business can afford to reduce and what resources must be maintained or possibly even increased. It must determine what areas have the greatest degree of productivity leverage and where the most effective changes can be made to improve productivity. Each industry may have different areas of greatest leverage. To understand how they differ, we must first understand their financial structure.

Industry Financial Characteristics: Magnitude of the Leverage

The Balance Sheet

Investment, financing, profitability, and cost patterns vary significantly from industry to industry. To determine what resources can be varied to increase productivity, reduce costs, and improve profitability, each company should analyze its balance sheet and then perform an out-of-pocket cost "sensitivity" analysis. The balance sheet will reveal the major areas of assets and liabilities.

Table 3–1 illustrates how such an analysis can be performed. The table presents the balance sheets of companies representing several types of industries: an equipment leasing company, a commercial bank, an electric utility, a supermarket chain, an advertising agency, and an au-

Table 3–1
Sample Balance Sheet Analysis

	Equipment Leasing	Commercial Bank	Electric Utility	Supermarket Chain	Advertising Agency	Auto Manu-facturer
Cash and marketable securities	9.4%	28.0%	0.2%	12.0%	18.0%	8.4%
Receivables	18.4	67.3	1.7	3.1	61.1	6.6
Inventories	6.5	—	1.4	39.5	—	25.1
Other current assets	—	0.4	0.6	3.0	8.9	3.9
Plant and equipment (net)	60.3	2.7	95.5	41.3	9.8	43.7
Other assets	5.4	1.6	0.6	1.1	2.2	12.3
Total assets	100.0	100.0	100.0	100.0	100.0	100.0
Notes payable	—	6.9	2.9	6.8	—	5.1
Accounts payable	4.4	77.3	0.8	25.0	46.4	23.7
Accrued taxes	8.2	—	0.5	1.0	2.3	3.6
Other current liabilities	1.9	5.2	1.7	7.3	10.1	0.7
Long-term debt	58.0	1.1	50.1	3.8	3.3	4.6
Other liabilities	4.3	2.5	2.4	3.8	—	7.1
Preferred stock	8.1	0.2	9.4	3.6	—	—
Capital stock and capital surplus	7.1	4.3	26.1	37.7	6.4	6.2
Retained earnings and reserves	8.0	2.5	6.1	14.8	31.5	49.0
Total liabilities and stockholder equity	100.0	100.0	100.0	100.0	100.0	100.0

tomobile manufacturer. Table 3–1 is by no means all-inclusive but is intended to demonstrate only that the areas of profitability leverage vary greatly from one business to another, and that a careful analysis of business sheets is a prerequisite to formulating a productivity strategy. These balance sheets reveal that the electric utility, equipment leasing, auto manufacturer, and supermarket chain are very capital-intensive. The commercial bank and advertising agency heavily depend on accounts receivable. The supermarket chain and auto manufacturer have large inventory investments and need to manage this asset prudently. Clearly the areas that need to be controlled most effectively vary a great deal from industry to industry.

In recent years, measurements such as ROCA (return on controllable assets) have been used to ascertain how effectively those assets that are actually controllable are being managed. Such measurements are valuable tools to determine the actions that should be taken to increase profits. The properly understood and intelligently compared use of well-known control tools such as ROCA, income statements, operating ratios, and financial ratios can provide valuable information for controlling costs. Using these tools, financial management must provide guidance to the rest of management in determining the areas of greatest leverage for increasing productivity and profits.

It would seem obvious that any astute business executive would study his balance sheet for clues on how to cut costs, save money, and increase profits. Unfortunately, many companies have embarked on exotic and well-publicized productivity programs, such as automation, with little understanding of the real effect that these ventures would have on their productivity. These tools have too often been adopted because it seemed like the right thing to do. But without a careful analysis of how and where these tools should be used and the probable payback resulting from their use, the results can be of little value. In some cases, they can be disastrous.

How Do We Know What Levers to Pull?

After the balance sheet is understood, we need to determine what levers must be pulled to achieve greatest profit and productivity. A great deal of money and management attention can be spent on the wrong levers with no increases in productivity. One method of determining where the leverage exists is to study out-of-pocket costs. From these costs, we can determine what changes in cost will result from variations in the major factors that make up the product cost. An industry's sensitivity to these changes will depend on the nature of the industry.

For a given industry and company, a simple set of calculations can identify what changes can be made to achieve substantial increases in productivity. These calculations can demonstrate that the most obvious choices may be wrong and even counterproductive.

A company's profit and loss statement, the cost structure, and a cost sensitivity analysis provide an excellent framework for taking the most potent actions to increase productivity. A sample profit and loss statement for a manufacturing company is outlined in table 3–2. The cost structure for U.S. manufacturing industries is shown in table 3–3 Note that direct labor costs almost never exceed 20 percent.

Using this cost structure, we can now analyze the sensitivity of changes in these cost factors to the total cost. A portion of the *other costs* category would be production engineering. In a company with a moderate amount of engineering, these costs would amount to approximately 8 to 40 percent of the total. Table 3–4 shows how much the total would be reduced by varying labor costs, engineering costs, and line throughput.

This analysis is theoretical and is based on the assumption that as each factor is varied, all other factors remain constant. In practice, this assumption is uncertain. This analysis also assumes that the factory is constrained—that is, it is fully utilized and additional demand exists to absorb an increase in production. This notwithstanding, our analysis will give us a reasonable approximation of the leverage on product cost for each factor.

Using the numbers from tables 3–2, 3–3, and 3–4, consider a prod-

Table 3–2
Sample Profit and Loss Statement

Net sales	$100
Cost of goods sold	60
Gross margin	$ 40
Selling, administrative, and research and development	25
Inventory carrying charges	5
Gross profit (pretax)	$ 10
Net profit	$ 5

Table 3–3
Cost of Goods Sold

Direct labor	4–20%
Other costs	80–96%

Table 3–4
Cost Sensitivity

	Percentage of Cost Reduction
25% reduction in direct labor	1–5%
25% reduction in engineering	2–5%
25% increase in line throughput	10–25%

uct that is sold for $100, with a manufacturing cost of $60. If the direct labor portion of this cost is 10 percent or $6.00, a 25 percent reduction of this direct labor would reduce the product cost by $1.50, or 1-1/2 percent of the sale price. This hardly represents a dramatic improvement in productivity.

The numbers in Tables 3–2, 3–3, and 3–4 are not precise and vary from company to company. Nevertheless, they demonstrate the structure of companies that have relatively low direct labor content, which is representative of almost the entire U.S. manufacturing industry.

What can be concluded from this analysis? First, a substantial reduction in direct labor, even when accompanied by no reduction in output, will have little effect on the cost of the product. In addition, reductions in the costs of engineering do not by themselves provide the largest cost improvements.

We certainly do not advocate high engineering and overhead costs as the key to improved productivity. But this analysis shows that the greatest leverage is obtained with increases in the amount of product a factory can produce—that is, its output—if we can achieve these increases with an incrementally small additional resource. Reductions in labor, engineering support, and overhead costs, if they are to have real major value, must be accompanied by an increase in output. Such significant increases in output can be achieved with a small increase in labor and tools, resulting in dramatic improvements in productivity and reduction in costs. Any company, whether it is manufacturing or nonmanufacturing, can perform a similar analysis of its operations and reveal major opportunities for improving productivity.

4
Unlocking the Productivity Potential: What Is the Key?

Despite the shift in the U.S. economy from manufacturing to services, manufacturing productivity is vital to economic prosperity. To achieve high productivity, to remain competitive, and to revitalize the U.S. economy, specific productivity techniques must be adopted. The methods we advocate can be applied successfully to practically any industry or business. They are not theoretical. The observations and productivity techniques discussed in this book are based on actual data and experience. Every stated productivity benefit has been demonstrated many times, in many places, with great success.

The U.S. economy has undergone two major transformations since the founding of the republic: two Industrial Revolutions. The first directed the economy's focus from agriculture to manufacturing; the second was an analogous move from manufacturing to the service industries. The second is sometimes referred to as a transformation to an information society because much of the growth in the service sector comes from service workers who are engaged in the creation, processing, and distribution of information. Some economic theorists have speculated that because of this shift to a service society, manufacturing industrial performance will be less important to the United States' economic future. We strongly disagree.

An excellent case for the importance of manufacturing productivity in the United States was made by the noted economist Lester C. Thurow in a recent article in *Newsweek:* "As the competitive decline of Industrial America has become more marked, service industries have increasingly come to be seen as America's economic salvation. . . . America is simply the first industrial country to enter the brave new age of the service economy. Service industries have been growing rapidly. In the five years from 1977 to 1982, services accounted for 62 percent of the growth in full-time equivalent workers in the private economy. But if one examines where this employment growth has occurred, it becomes clear that service employment is neither likely to continue growing at the current rate nor likely to be a route to future prosperity." After Thurow points out that such growth service industries as health care, legal services, and business services such as accounting are limited in their potential growth, he concludes that "Like it or not, if American industry goes down the tubes, most of the rest of us will go down with it."[1]

John R. Opel, IBM chairman, considers manufacturing productivity fundamental to the success of his company. Opel has declared four goals for IBM in the 1980s: first, "to grow with the industry"; second, "to exhibit product leadership across our entire product line—to excel in technology, value and quality"; third, "to be the most efficient in everything we do—to be the low-cost producer, the low-cost servicer, the low-cost administrator"; and fourth, "to sustain our profitability, which funds our growth."[2]

The survival of U.S. business will be determined by the performance of manufacturing, agriculture, mining, and other activities that produce goods. If the United States produces in a highly effective way, it will compete and prosper. If it doesn't produce, it will, in Thurow's words, "go down the tubes."

Computers and telecommunications will be two of the world's largest industries in the 1990s, which is why this book focuses on basic methods by which large gains can be attained in these industries. Many books on productivity study the automobile industry. Although we have chosen high technology to demonstrate the versatility of our productivity techniques, most of these methods are equally suited and, in fact, easier to apply to the rest of the industry. Furthermore, once the techniques discussed in this book are understood for the environment of the complexity of high technology, their application to the rest of industry is relatively straightforward.

The Bureau of Labor Statistics has reported that high technology companies have research and development expenditures and numbers of technical employees that are twice as high as the average of all U.S. manufacturing.[3] High technology will certainly include the technologies of information processing (computers, semiconductors, software, data processing, computer-aided design, manufacturing), communications (telephones, satellites, television), robots, biotechnology, electronics, medical and optical instruments and equipment, fiber optics, and vapor-phase technology—in short, activities that will continue to have an enormous effect on all phases of U.S. business.

Despite increasing sales, U.S. producers of high technology products have discovered that generating sufficient cash to continue expanding and upgrading their production capacities will not be easy because of the increasing capital-intensive nature of the industry. Moreover, technology is changing at an astonishingly rapid pace. In this environment, U.S. industry must adopt two strategies:

Increase capacity utilization to meet increasing demand as well as to become the low-cost producer; and

Maintain a flexible manufacturing capability that adapts to the fast-changing manufacturing environment.

For these reasons, we have focused on many productivity techniques that will increase capacity utilization in any industry.

5
Innovation and Technology

The Biggest Contributor to Productivity

Innovation is a major contributor to achieving leadership in the international productivity race. But the United States must change its concept of what constitutes innovation. U.S. industry must recognize that if it is to capitalize on its immense innovative capability, it must make many changes in the way it manages, finances, plans, and implements new products and technologies. It must explore new methods of organization, new concepts of financing, new skills, different methods of motivating and rewarding its employees, and different ways of planning. The management of industrial enterprises, boards of directors, and millions of stockholders must learn that there is a major difference between a profit this year and sustained growth for ten or fifteen years in the future.

The relationship between product developers and manufacturers is vital to the achievement of long-term growth in this new area of advanced technologies and products. What is done with this relationship and how it is managed will strongly influence how the United States succeeds in bringing its products from the invention stage to the marketplace. But the partnership between these two important parts of any company is only part of the answer. All parts of the company play a vital role in achieving success: those who participate in the financial decisions on how much to spend and when and where to spend it, those responsible for hiring, training, and organization, and the marketing arm. Every part of the company must act in concert with every other part. They must collectively act as a system. Management must have the necessary knowledge of the business and management skill to orchestrate all of these parts in such a way that the business works effectively and quickly.

According to the Brookings Institution, 44 percent of U.S. productivity improvement is due to technological innovation.[1] If the portion of U.S. productivity improvement attributable to technology innovation is so large, what is all the fuss about?

According to D. Bruce Merrifield, assistant secretary of commerce for productivity, technology, and innovation, "In just this last 30-year period, something like 90 percent of all scientific knowledge has been generated. This pool will double again in the next 10 or 15 years. Of course, 90 percent of all the scientists who have ever lived are now living and working, and they will double again in that period." What role has the United States played in this technology explosion? According to Merrifield, "The United States a decade ago, with only 5 percent of the world's population, was generating something like 75 percent of the world's technology. Now the U.S. share is about 50 percent. In another decade, it may be 30 percent, not because we're generating less—we'll be generating a great deal more—but because the other 95 percent of the world will also be contributing."[2]

Despite breathtaking U.S. advances, Japan is moving at even a more rapid pace. In some fields, such as silicon integrated memories, Japan has not only caught up with the United States, it has actually passed it. In practically every field Japan has undertaken, whether it is semiconductors, computers, or automobiles, it has started from well behind U.S. industry, approached it, and in many cases assumed leadership in the worldwide technology race.

The United States has always prided itself on being more inventive than any nation in the world, including Japan. It has always believed that although Japan has done a good job copying U.S. products, it is not as innovative. The major innovations of the postwar industrial era have come from the United States, not Japan. Americans invented computers, automation, robots, and electronics. The United States has expended astronomical sums of money on research and development, far more than any nation on earth, including Japan. If Americans are the innovators, how can they possibly fall behind?

The answer lies in some misconceptions, even myths, about the real nature of innovation. In the first place, the most dramatic of inventions, no matter how advanced the theory or exotic its technology, will have no commercial value if it never reaches the marketplace. Even if it reaches the marketplace, it may not help competitiveness if it arrives several years later than a competitor's version.

To maintain U.S. competitiveness in world markets, two seemingly obvious conditions must be satisfied. First, technological innovations must be proven "manufacturable"; they must be produced at a high level of quality and reproducibility and at a low cost. Second, production must be achieved in the shortest space of time. Unless these two conditions are met, the United States really isn't being innovative. To the scientific community, technical papers in learned journals describing the theory of operation of a bold new invention may be very exciting and reflect justifiable credit to the inventor. But this innovation will have absolutely no effect on overall national productivity unless it is manufacturable at a low cost and with high quality. Even if these goals are achieved, they will not improve industrial competitiveness if they are accomplished several years after the United States' international competitors. Furthermore, expending increasingly vast amounts of money on research will have little effect on productivity if the art of manufacturability is not mastered. Even massive increases in capital will not, by itself, solve U.S. problems. After all, astronomical capital expenditures during the last ten to twenty years have not resulted in significant increases in U.S. productivity.

Robert Hayes and William Abernathy provide further insights to U.S. productivity:

> To an unprecedented degree, success in most industries today requires an organizational commitment to compete in the marketplace on technological grounds—that is, to compete over the long run by offering superior products. Yet, guided by what they took to be the newest and best principles of management, American managers have increasingly directed their attention elsewhere. These new principles, despite their sophistication and widespread usefulness . . . encourage a preference for (1) analytic detachment rather than the insight that comes from "hands on" experience and (2) short-term cost reduction rather than long-term development of technological competitiveness. It is this new management gospel, we feel, that has played a major role in undermining the vigor of American industry. . . . American business today is making small, short-term adjustments by cutting costs and by turning to the government for temporary relief. . . . Success in trade is the result of patient and meticulous preparations with a long period of market preparation before the rewards are available.[3]

In other words, vast investments in research and development will result in little improvement in the United States' productivity and competitive position if it is not prepared to follow the course of "patient and meticulous preparations." The U.S. industrial penchant for closely monitoring and measuring quarterly earnings achievements has resulted in short-term profit growth, improved short-term stock prices, but long-term industrial stagnation.

The record of U.S. industry certainly demonstrates that technical innovation has produced some major gains in productivity. Table 1–1 showed how new technology in the past dramatically reduced the cost of data processing. These radical reductions in cost and improvements in performance during the last twenty to thirty years were the direct result of technological changes from the vacuum tube and ferrite cores to large-scale integrated circuits and thin film disk storage. Furthermore, this dramatic impact on productivity affected almost the entire electronics industry. Spectacular price reductions of watches, calculators, high-fidelity equipment, videocassette recorders, and microprocessors are everyday examples of the impact of technology innovation on productivity.

In fact, the influence of technological innovation on productivity can be demonstrated in practically every industry whether it is high technology, electronic circuitry, or fast food hamburgers. Despite these dramatic examples, technological innovation still has had relatively little impact on overall national productivity improvement when compared with other nations.

Because much if not most of this meteoric improvement in technology was accomplished in the United States, can it be concluded that the United States has nothing to worry about? The answer is a resounding no. A runner can easily win a race if he has no opposition. For many years during the postwar era, while much of the world was recovering from the economic ravages of World War II, the United States had the field to itself. Its industrial accomplishments were awesome, and there was little threat to U.S. supremacy. U.S. technical innovations were translated into products for the marketplace, but the United States essentially performed these miracles at its own pace and achieved major productivity advantages over other nations.

Today the race is changing. The United States no longer has token opposition. Not only are the Japanese achieving equality in technological know-how, they are achieving it at a rapid pace. Historically, high technology producers in the United States have taken seven to nine years to manufacture products that were introduced by the research laboratories; today Japan is performing this feat in two to three years. This ability to translate technological innovation into the marketplace faster than any other nation is the single largest reason for Japanese productivity performance.

If the past enormous U.S. research and development expenditures are compared with Japanese performance, it is clear that so far no direct correlation exists between the level of technological innovation produced by a country and its ability to implement it. To successfully achieve manufacturability of technology requires the "meticulous preparations" described by Hayes and Abernathy. Furthermore, these preparations do not come at bargain basement prices. Attempts by industry to short-circuit these preparations in order to satisfy short-term bottom line objectives will result in calamity for U.S. industry. As technology becomes more advanced, it becomes more difficult and demanding, and its importance continues to increase.

Managing Technological Change

To understand how management of new products and technologies must change requires first understanding how these products themselves have changed. Forty thousand years ago, the most advanced technology was the flint arrowhead, designed and produced by one man, with the crudest of tools and an unrefined set of processes. The specifications were all in his head, and the manufacturing processes completely in his hands. He conceived of, developed, and manufactured his product by himself. He was a one-man organization. There was no staff, no overhead, no need to hold meetings and issue procedures. For many thousands, even tens of thousands of years, most products and the techniques to build them were simple, and the organizations to develop and build them consisted of one, or at most, a few people, tools, and possibly one or two oxen.

As products became more complex, the process of designing them, specifying their size, their shape, and the materials required to build them became more complex. The invention, development, and production of these products involved many people. One person did not possess the diversity of skills, knowledge, energy, or time to do the job alone. Organizations were formed to cope with this diversity and with the need to effectively manage the larger resource requirements for the job. The methods of organization became a science, and new techniques were developed to cope with this new challenge.

With the advent of the Industrial Revolution, the sewing machine, steam engine, the wireless, and eventually the automobile led the way to increasing complexity. New engineering disciplines were created, and the era of the chemical, industrial, mechanical, and electrical engineer was born. Groups were created to invent, to develop, and to manufacture these new products. The inventor passed a concept to a design engineer. The design engineer produced a design and set of specifications. The manufacturer took these specifications and built prototypes, perhaps performed some minor redesign, and finally built the product. During the engineering phase of this work, chemical, electrical, and mechanical specialists became essential to ensure that by using their skills a good design would result.

As industry progressed, methods of organization progressed, too, and eventually resulted in the idea of a "functional" organization. Research was performed by scientists and inventors. Development laboratories staffed with trained technical specialists generated new product designs from ideas introduced by the research laboratories. Manufacturing operations built the tools, and hired and trained the workers who built the products.

This traditional method of organization has undergone many variations but continues to dominate today. Has it worked? It certainly has. The United States' vast industrial growth and leadership in industry proves that it has worked. Then why should we change? If something isn't broken, why fix it? The reason for change lies in the nature of the products of today and the future.

The products and technologies of today and tomorrow range from the simplest, a toothpick, to the very complex, such as the semiconductor integrated circuit. Between these extremes lies a massive array of products and technologies, and as time passes, far more products approach the integrated circuit in complexity. Certain facts characterize the higher technologies that distinguish them from the simple mechanical products of the past. Modern products are built with a combination of chemical, metallurgical, and mechanical processes. Highly sophisticated electronic, optical, and mechanical tools are used to perform these processes. Measurement systems of the most advanced electrical, mechanical, and optical technologies are required to monitor and measure the progress of the manufacturing process and the results when it is completed. Computers are used to guide, record, control, and measure during the product design and production process. People must operate and interact with the processes and the tools. The room environment must be specified and controlled, often to exceedingly high levels of cleanliness and low levels of humidity. Engineers, technicians, administrators, and production control experts must work in close contact with and in synchronization with the tools, processes, and computers. In other words, the manufacture of many if not most products today requires the control and management of a total *system* of people, tools, materials, processes, and even the factory environment. Even the safety of the worker is part of the system. Every part of that system interacts with every other part. If the individual pieces of the system are designed separately and operated independently, the system won't work.

A system is defined as "a regularly interacting or interdependent group of items forming a unified whole."[4] Probably the most complex example of a system is the human body. If the human body had been created by a group of specialists and a functional organization, we probably wouldn't be around today to read or write this book. Consider an organization headed by a general manager with a manager for each of the following departments: brain, stomach, heart, circulatory system, lungs, and digestive tract. All managers are dedicated to excel in their own areas of expertise and to produce the best possible product in each of their respective categories. Assume that the management team meets once a week to discuss administrative matters and also enjoys brief and pleasant conversations at Christmas parties and occasional company picnics. Assume that at the end of the planned development period the results are superb. Each manager has been motivated with the expectation of a large bonus that would result from the development of the products to specification. The general manager could point to a series of independent achievements of great magnitude. Everybody would be rewarded for a job well done. The only problem with this scenario would be the final result. When the top executive assembled the pieces, the body would be lifeless.

Unfortunately, this analogy applies all too well to industry today. Not only are U.S. industrial organizations run as a series of independent, uncoordinated pieces, but management motivates and pays people to operate that way. We encourage individual accomplishment. We hold in high esteem the high scorer, the prolific inventor, the Nobel prize winner, the opera superstar. Few rewards are given for cooperating with a colleague, sharing information, or working diligently with a group of fellow contributors with the objective of success for the total collective venture. This worship of individuality and individual accomplishment is not all bad. It has made the United States the most creative nation on earth and has brought it great rewards. But individuality has its price. The type of high technology world that has emerged during the past twenty years, and the accelerating pace of development that can be expected in the future, have taught that recognition of individual achievement alone can have serious handicaps. If the complex products of the future are really systems, then they must be developed as systems and by using an organizational system to perform the development.

Let's look at a typical product that is built with a combination of metals, chemicals, tools, people, and the basic materials from which the product is formed. Examples of such a product would be a semiconductor integrated chip, a magnetic disk, or an electronic package. An engineer designs the product by describing the materials with which it will be built, and the chemical and metallurgical processes by which it will modify the size, dimensions, or even the composition of the materials. He will specify the dimensions, tolerances, and electrical or mechanical performance of the product. Then he will make a few models to verify that the design is approximately workable and the models will function. What if he discovers, to his chagrin, that the model won't work? What will he do next? He calls the metallurgist to find out if the metallurgical composition that was specified was correct. The metallurgist answers, "I followed your specification to the letter; I am not the one to blame." Perhaps there are problems with the testing equipment; the equipment could have made a false reading and inaccurately characterized the true performance of the model. The test engineer answers that it can't possibly be so: "I checked everything out before I made the tests; I am not to blame." Perhaps one of the chemical solvents used in the cleaning operations was contaminated; the vendor of the chemical must be selling substandard solvent. The purchasing agent contacts the vendor who answers that the solvent precisely meets the specifications requested. In frustration, the design engineer makes some changes in the design, revises some of the materials specifications, builds more models, and again meets with failure.

The next approach is to call a meeting of the metallurgist, test engineer, purchasing agent, and experts in other specialties. Half of the invitees appear at the meeting; the other half, pleading pressure of other commitments and feeling no interest or responsibility in the design engineer's problem, stay away. The meeting, lasting only the hour allowed for it under pressure of other schedules, results in finger pointing, few new ideas, considerable frustration, and little progress. The design engineer is forced to continue a fruitless cycle of trial and error, hoping to find the combination to a very complex puzzle, if not by scientific means, perhaps by some accident of good fortune.

What went wrong? How could failure occur when every engineer involved in this work—the chemist, the metallurgist, the mechanical engineer, the test engineer, and the purchasing agent—was a well-trained, competent person with many years of experience solving difficult technical problems? The first reason is that none of them had any commitment to or interest in the job. They were being paid to be good engineers, to excel in their disciplines, but they had little motivation to solve this particular problem. They were probably involved in many other projects. They were under great time pressures and could devote little time to each. Furthermore, the design engineer who ostensibly was in charge of the program to design this product had little influence over others' actions and was dependent entirely on powers of persuasion, diplomatic ability, and maybe some intervention from higher levels of management.

Now let's look at a different way of getting the job done. The design engineer is put in direct charge of the program. For the next six months, the chemist, metallurgist, purchasing agent, and electrical engineer are temporarily taken from their parent organizations and placed under the direct technical supervision of the design engineer. Of course, this move is made after a considerable amount of contention among those in various levels of management who do not want to surrender any territory. But top management prevails, the move is made, and the engineering team goes to work. All members are informed that their next raise depends solely on the success of the program to which they are now assigned. After the first experimental models are unsuccessfully made, the group assembles to diagnose the problem. The design engineer now has the undivided attention of the group. Former allegiances are forgotten, and they all concentrate on one objective. The design engineer is recognized as the true leader, and personal economic interest motivates all. Furthermore, the problems are challenging.

The group soon recognizes that the product they are developing is more complicated than they originally realized. Some of the metals they deposited on the base material would not adhere properly. Not only do they have to modify the metallurgy, they also need to change some of the physical characteristics of the surface of the base material so that this metal will adhere to it and maintain certain dimensional specifications. The only way they can achieve the required surface characteristics is to carry out a chemical etching process. This process requires a change in the equipment used to perform the etch. Next they discover that the dimensions of some of the features on the surface of the material are so small and the tolerances so minute that they must revise the design of the product to facilitate their ability to successfully carry out the metallurgical deposition process. Next they realize that the probes used to contact the surface for electrical tests must be redesigned to permit the test equipment to make contact with the newly revised metallurgy.

What this group is learning is that practically every problem it faces in redesigning the product interacts with many of the other problems and that the solutions require a total system solution. By designing a set of experiments to carefully evaluate each change in design and process, and by working closely together to understand the effect of each of these changes, the group finds that total solution. They succeed because of synergism—"cooperative action of discrete agencies such that the total effect is greater than the sum of the effects taken independently."[5]

What the members of this group have done is to recognize the systems nature of the product. They merged their skills and thought processes. They complemented each other in a way that independent action would never succeed in doing. Furthermore, they were driven by a common leader, a common goal, and an important motivating force, reward for success of the project.

Not only did they succeed in achieving a successful design, but they succeeded much faster. They solved their problems in parallel, not in series. They greatly reduced the false starts and blind alleys into which the independent mode would have led them. Their decisions for each stage of the development process were made on rational thought, not on a series of intuitive stabs at a quick solution.

After the group achieves success, can it assume that the job is done? It has achieved a product design with a set of tools and processes to build it. Does it now write a set of specifications describing how it built the product, hand the specifications to the production management, pride itself on a job well done, and proceed to start developing the next product? Far from it. Proof of the existence of a workable product in the development laboratory is the beginning, not the conclusion, of the product development process.

Some common misconceptions exist about how a new design is moved from the laboratory to the factory floor. Some of the reasons for these misconceptions lie in history—a history of successfully doing it an old and traditional way. What is the traditional way, and why has it worked?

Most development and manufacturing operations rely on a development function to design and prove the feasibility of making a product to its performance specifications. The development engineer writes a set of specifications that the manufacturing function copies to build and reproduce the product in high volume. The design of a simple mechanical device can be described by specifying the material to be used, and by a drawing describing its shape, dimensions, and tolerances. It may even include some heat treatment procedures and possibly some methods of cleaning. The design of this device can be relatively simple and will not be difficult to produce. Standard machines can work the material to achieve the shape, dimensions, and tolerances in repeatable fashion. There is little doubt that the design furnished by the development group can be reproduced by an independent manufacturing operation. Little communication is required between the development laboratory and production once the design is fully understood by the manufacturing personnel. Some early discussion may be called for between the two functions, and possibly some design changes, but this period should be brief.

As products have become more complex, increasing interaction has been needed among the various parts of the product. The meshing of two or more gears, for example, needs control of dimensions and tolerances and places great demands on the gear material to assure reliability and reduction of wear during operation. This increased complexity places a greater need for interaction between the development engineer and the manufacturer. The manufacturing engineer must have some influence over the design to be sure that design tolerances and materials properties are consistent with good manufacturing control. There must be a close working relationship between the design engineer and his manufacturing engineering counterpart to assure adequate discussion and cooperation needed to produce a manufacturable design. In other words, the design of the product, the process by which it is reduced to a physical model, and the reproduction of that model in manufacturing require very close collaboration and synergism among the various parties involved in these activities. To the extent that this collaboration must exist, it is up to the individual parties to rise above their individual interests in favor of the main objective—to develop and manufacture the product. Often this joint effort occurs naturally, as a result of the relationships set up informally by the concerned parties. Sometimes the individual people recognize that this is an important part of their function, and often these responsibilities are formally spelled out in job descriptions. Where these motivations are still insufficient, higher management, recognizing what is needed to get the job done, will step in to ensure that those people with the required skills get together to solve the problems.

But what happens as the complexity of the problems increases further? The semiconductor integrated chip is a good example. This high technology product is built with two or three hundred individual process steps. As semiconductor technology progresses, the steps increase not only in number but also in difficulty. Dimensions and tolerances, already microscopic, decrease further. The exposure to defects from the most infinitesimal contaminants becomes steadily larger. The interactions between and among process steps increases. The product becomes a complex system of many layers of oxides, metals, chemicals, glasses, polymers, and solvents. Features on the surface of submicroscopic dimensions are formed by space-age techniques such as ion implantation, diffusion, oxidation, vapor-deposition, and electron beam and photo-optical exposure. The design, process development, proof of reproducibility and reliability, and finally the mass production of these products require a level of technical and management mastery unequalled in any previous age.

6
Why Hasn't the U.S. Game Plan Worked?

If you Care about Productivity, Examine Your CARE Strategy

Every economist knows that the major solution to U.S. economic problems is to substantially increase productivity. Numerous books and articles during the past few years have provided a constant drumbeat about its importance and all of the great things that the United States is doing about it. But how well *are* we doing? One indicator of economic health is the trend in the average real earnings of the U.S. worker, not just the dollars in the paycheck but the purchasing power of these dollars. Table 6–1, published by the U.S. Bureau of Labor Statistics, generally regarded as authoritative, answers the question. According to the table, most Americans have not increased their purchasing power since 1970. In fact, with the exception of a few mining workers, at least for those who have been able to keep their jobs, the real earnings in every other industrial group either virtually remained unchanged or actually fell.

Another way to measure the U.S. economy's performance is to compare the improvements in manufacturing productivity in the United States with improvements by several other industrial powers. Table 6–2 makes this comparison. More recent data from Robert J. Gordon of Northwestern University shows that during the years 1979 to 1984 manufacturing productivity in the United States continued at approximately the same average rate of annual growth, 2.5 percent, that had been achieved during the previous twenty years.[1] It has been no secret that the United States has lagged behind Japan in productivity growth for several years. What is surprising, however, is that our growth lags behind the major industrial nations of western Europe by at least a factor of 2 to 1.

Economists, business executives, academicians, government officials, and politicians have all contributed to the long list of explanations, or in some cases, excuses for the U.S. productivity crisis. Table 6–3 lists examples of these reasons in two categories—favorable (those that improve productivity) and unfavorable (those that result in declining productivity).

Table 6–1
Weekly Earnings by Industry Group, 1970–1982

	Current Dollars						Constant (1977) Dollars					
	1970	1975	1979	1980	1981	1982ᵃ	1970	1975	1979	1980	1981	1982ᵃ
Gross weekly earnings	$120	$164	$220	$235	$255	$267	$187	$185	$183	$173	$170	$167
Manufacturing	134	191	269	289	318	334	209	215	224	212	212	209
Mining	164	249	365	397	439	462	256	280	304	292	293	289
Construction	195	266	343	368	399	428	304	300	286	270	266	268
Transportation, public utilities	156	233	326	351	382	398	243	262	272	258	255	249
Wholesale trade	137	183	248	267	292	309	214	206	207	197	195	193
Retail trade	82	109	139	147	158	165	128	123	116	108	105	103
Finance, insurance, real estate	113	148	191	210	229	242	176	167	159	154	153	151
Services	97	135	175	191	209	223	151	152	146	140	139	140

Source: U.S. Bureau of Labor Statistics.
ᵃAs of June 1982.

Table 6–2
Average Annual Rates of Change of Major Industrial
Economies, 1960–1980

	Productivity Growth
Japan	9.3%
Italy	5.9
France	5.5
Federal Republic of Germany	5.4
Canada	3.8
United Kingdom	3.2
United States	2.7

Source: U.S. Bureau of Labor Statistics.

The many books and articles on productivity motivate the public to think about the issue, but they do little or nothing to increase productivity. A debate on each item in table 6–3 would probably reveal that some of the items really do help or hurt productivity. But the debate would also disclose that many of the unfavorable items are irrelevant and are merely excuses for U.S. industry to avoid developing constructive ways to solve the problem.

The Unfulfilled Promise of CARE

Over the last two decades U.S. industry has attempted to exploit four areas of innovation and growth that supposedly hold the key to a rapid productivity explosion. These areas appear on almost everyone's list of favorite productivity tools. In this book, these four factors are referred to as CARE:

C̲omputers/information systems

A̲utomation

R̲obotics

E̲lectronics

What has become of the promise of CARE? Table 6–2 indicates that the United States has not been completely successful in applying these tools. Are there fundamental limitations in their application? Have they been misapplied? Has U.S. industry been misled by their glamour?

Table 6–3
Factors Commonly Believed to Influence Productivity

Favorable	Unfavorable
Increased capital, investment in plant equipment and process	Management's ineffectiveness
Increase in research and development expenditures	Government regulations
	Lack of management commitment and involvement
Management commitment and involvement	Inadequate training of management supervisors and work force
Nonunionization	High taxation
Improved personnel relations: better communication, worker involvement, labor/management participation	High inflation
	High energy costs
	Uncertain economic conditions
Increased savings rate	Poor worker attitudes: lack of motivation, declining work ethic, militancy
Improved depreciation and investment tax credit programs	
Effective engineering/manufacturing interface in product/process design	Unionization
	Shift to service-oriented economy
Increased automation/mechanization	Short-term growth/profit orientation
Increased use of robots	
Increased use of computers/information systems	Poor/outmoded product and process design
Increased use of electronics	High average age of plant and equipment
Quality circles/quality focus	Individual-oriented society
State-of-the-art product and process engineering	Poor planning
	Lack of worker involvement
Long-term growth/profit orientation	Lack of productivity objectives/goals/programs
Reduction of labor content	Antitrust laws
Focus on detail	
Government subsidies	
High market share/economics of scale	
Group-company-oriented society	
Innovation and creativity	
Technical excellence	
Incentive programs/awards	
Implementation of production standards	
Emphasis on methods improvement	
Cooperative/loyal work force	
Government sponsorship of productivity programs	
Lifetime employment/job security	
Long-term performance evaluation	
Consensus or bottoms-up decision making	

CARE: The Role of Computers/Information Systems

A computer is a versatile electronic product that performs a wide range of functions. According to the editors of *PC Retailing* magazine, "Basically it processes words or numbers, manipulates lists, and stores and retrieves information of all sorts."[2]

The semiconductor integrated circuit is the basis for the phenomenal growth of the computer market. Without the integrated silicon circuit, computers as they are known today would be impossible. The cost, performance, and density of computers have improved explosively since the introduction of the transistorized computer in the late 1950s. By packing more and more transistors into the same quarter-inch-square chip of silicon, the price of electronic circuitry has decreased dramatically. During the eighteen years from 1960 to 1979, the price for the simplest electronic circuit dropped from nearly $10 to only one-tenth of a cent. The density of integrated circuits leaped from 50 transistors on a chip of silicon to 1,000 in the 1970s to an astronomical 500,000. By the 1990s the density will have reached a stratospheric 20 million transistors. The cost of the simplest of electronic circuits is projected to be less than one-thousandth of a cent. The improvement of productivity of the semiconductor industry is unrivaled in the history of manufacturing. These phenomenal advances have brought about the incredible growth of the computer itself.

The productivity of manufacturing the computer has increased greatly, but what has the computer itself contributed to the advancement of productivity in industry in general? The applications of computers in business are too numerous to name. Enormous productivity gains in the office are clearly the result of the computer. Business applications such as budgeting, planning, accounts payable and receivable, payroll, word processing, electronic filing, electronic mail, order entry, billing, and invoicing have brought about a radical improvement in office productivity.

The influence of the computer on the factory floor has also been great. The computer became a major manufacturing tool in the mid-1960s, and its use increased dramatically throughout the next two decades. Processing of bills of materials, inventory control, purchasing, and computer-aided design and computer-aided manufacturing (CAD/CAM) all benefited from the computer.

Manufacturing resource planning (MRP) became the most popular manufacturing software application. The use of the computers in MRP has been widely advertised as the key to productivity in manufacturing. MRP becomes particularly valuable when a large number of part numbers are to be manufactured or purchased. The purpose of MRP is to develop for each part number the quantity required and the due date. The value of the computer is its ability to develop these production schedules rapidly and accurately. As the product line becomes more complex and the number of part numbers increases to the hundreds and thousands, the computer becomes an essential tool for increasing productivity. Without it, performing this work manually would become astronomically expensive, and subject to much error. The computer does calculations almost infinitely faster than a manual substitute. This seems to constitute an almost infinite improvement in productivity.

If the major application of computers in manufacturing has been the materials requirement system, and if the computer has enormously simplified and accelerated these operations, why has overall manufacturing productivity shown so little improvement? The answer lies in how the system is used. The problem lies in the information used in the system. The MRP system compares the product requirements with the capacity of the production line. If the capacity numbers are over- or understated, the system won't work and the calculations will be wrong. The computer is not at fault; it is doing its job rapidly and reliably. But all it is doing is obtaining inaccurate and useless information faster.

If the MRP system is operating with inadequate production capacity to execute MRP schedules, the system can become a nightmare. *The imbalance between the schedules and the actual capacity has been a primary cause of poor productivity performance.* This imbalance is created by inaccurate assumptions of the factors making up the calculation of capacity. The power of the computerized MRP system can be great if our planning assumptions are realistic. But the computer will not fix the chaotic problems that are created by using the wrong assumptions. According to Moshe Eliyahu Goldratt, founder of Creative Output, Inc., "The estimated $10 billion plus spent in the last 30 years to plan the flow of material through factories in an attempt to boost productivity has largely been a waste of money."[3]

Two important facts are emphasized many times in this book: First, increased utilization of capacity of U.S. plant and equipment is fundamental to successfully increased productivity; second, very realistic planning is a prerequisite for making the necessary decisions and taking the required actions to better use our capacity. These two points may appear to be obvious. But we demonstrate that not only are they extremely important but, also they are in fact usually ignored. We also describe powerful techniques that can help industry accomplish these objectives of realistic planning and higher capacity to achieve higher productivity.

Another area in which the computer is playing a major role in improving manufacturing productivity is computer-aided design (CAD) and computer-aided manufacturing (CAM). A combination of applications popularly known as CAD/CAM. CAD/CAM is used in either the design or the manufacturing of a product. CAD systems employ sophisticated computer graphics technology for applications that include printed circuit design, schematic design, and parts engineering. Three-dimensional scale representations of products created on a CAD system are sometimes translated directly into physical form through the automatic transfer of programmed specifications to a computer-aided manufacturing system controlling the operation of production equipment.

Other related areas of computer application include computer-aided engineering and computer-aided testing. At least two dozen software vendors have major offerings in these areas and extensive literature that describes the capabilities of their systems. The productivity benefits in the areas of engineering, mechanized design, drafting, and testing are very large. These applications will become not only commonplace but indispensable in many manufacturing industries.

The computer has played a major role in inventory management and control. Inventory systems are typically used for analyzing demand, forecasting sales, establishing order quantities, setting reorder points, and calculating safety stock. Actual use of these systems since 1962 has demonstrated that where inventories are a significant factor, major benefits can be realized in increased service to customers, reduction in inventories, and improved management control. The reduction in lead times for purchasing parts and manufacturing the product will continue to be a major factor in improving productivity. Reducing the costs of inventory and getting to the marketplace are all important objectives. As products and technologies become more complex and production processes increase in number, the reduction of cycle time becomes critical for achieving productivity gains.

Two other areas—application software and information—have been greatly influenced by the computer and are major factors in the future of U.S. productivity. But if they are the key to productivity, have they met their promise?

Computer application software is a set of custom instructions that a user inserts into a computer to serve his needs. The growth of this software has been absolutely staggering. According to *Software News* magazine (January 1983), the market for application software is expected to grow in 1983 for mainframe computers at an annual rate of 30 to 40 percent; for the minicomputer, 50 to 60 percent; and for microcomputers, 70 to 80 percent. The average application backlog for the mainframe computer is running between nine and ten months. The minicomputer users are experiencing delays averaging five to six months, and microcomputer users are waiting three to four months. Backlogs are expected to increase, and software costs are soaring.

These statistics are impressive. But more software does not necessarily result in greater productivity. In fact, the overall U.S. record indicates that despite the skyrocketing use of EDP and its associated software, productivity barely remains constant. The computer has been properly heralded as a major productivity tool, yet its increasing use has not resulted in any significant improvement in overall U.S. productivity. We expend a tremendous amount of energy and money to exploit these revolutionary technologies, but what do we get in return?

Should we conclude that since the expenditures of all this effort is not improving our productivity, we should reduce it? On the contrary, the potential productivity benefits of the application of computers to business, industry, and government is enormous. The problem is not in the generation of the software or in the machines themselves. Rather, the problem lies in what we do with computers. Measuring the number of lines of code, or the volume or height of all the paper a factory generates, is of little value. To what end is all this application software directed?

This staggering growth has resulted in an information explosion— or has it? It is not at all clear whether we have witnessed an information explosion or a data explosion. Data are merely facts; data may or may not be useful. If data is converted to potential usefulness, data can become information. Hundreds of pages of computer printouts with millions of numbers from a census can be worthless unless something useful is done with those numbers. In fact, the more data generated, the less useful that data may become. If all data can be put into some form that can be used, the data become information. If we can then put this information to practical use, it becomes knowledge.

Of what value are data and information if we do not have the knowledge to use them? Computers have accomplished what would have been impossible without them: they have made possible the highly productive availability of astronomical amounts of data and information. However, it isn't at all clear whether this availability has always been translated into knowledge of practical value. According to some estimates, scientific and technical information has been doubling in less than five years. Certainly U.S. productivity is not increasing at that rate.

The generation of this vast amount of unused data often has been called data pollution. It may not be dangerous to personal health; it does not kill fish like acid rain nor does it cause respiratory problems like industrial air pollution. But it can create serious health problems for an economy. The generation of mammoth amounts of unused data and information can create the illusion that we are increasing our productivity. But if we can convert data into knowledge, the power of the computer will increase enormously. (See chapters 8 to 12 for a review of some powerful techniques for the increase of productivity: how the translation of data collected by computers or other means can result in specific knowledge that, in turn, instructs us in how we must act to increase productivity.)

The computer or the software or the data do not by themselves result in the productivity improvements. The generation of volumes of data may do little to improve productivity and reduce costs. But computers properly directed can be a powerful force in making productivity advances. It is the knowledge created by the availability of all of the data that leads to correct decisions and actions. These advances can take place in the office or on the factory floor.

CARE: Does Automation Increase Productivity?

Hardly a week goes by without some national magazine or newspaper heralding the wonders of futuristic automatic factories operated with robots and controlled by computers. The specter of thousands, perhaps millions, of people thrown out of work by automation is raised with increasing frequency. We hear warnings of giant dislocations in U.S. society. According to these predictions, this new era will require radical changes in the educational system: it must retrain massive numbers of people who are educationally obsolete and who must learn the new technologies required to work in this new world. As thought-provoking as these observations may be, the bleak image of the future is overstated.

The trend toward industrial automation is indeed proceeding at an accelerating rate. Automation will play a major part in U.S. industry. It is not at all certain, however, how fast this movement toward automatic factories will occur. In some industries where simple assembly operations are predominant, the economic advantages and technical simplicity of automation may be clear. In more complex industries such as high technology (computers, semiconductors, and telecommunications), many problems may weigh strongly against too rapid a trend toward complete automation.

Automation is the term used to describe automatic operation and control of a process and equipment. It is automatic if it operates independently of external influence or control. It is self-regulating. The heating system in some homes is self-regulating. A thermostat tells the furnace when it must shut off or turn on; no human interaction is involved except to occasionally change the temperature limits to which the thermostat responds. This heating system is very simple. It consists of one sector, the furnace, and one sensor, the thermostat. For a simple industrial process that contains one, or at most a few sectors, some form of automation can be technically and economically feasible. As the production line becomes more complex, though, automation as we have defined it becomes more difficult. (See the case study on Autotech in Chapter 13 for a description of such a production line.)

According to Moshe Eliyahu Goldratt, "A good chunk of the billions of dollars invested in 'factory of the future' equipment at company after company in the U.S. is either misspent or entirely unnecessary."[4] The decisions about whether and when to automate are often based on misunderstandings about what automation can in fact do. Management usually automates because it wants its factories to be more efficient, productive, and competitive. The most common perception is that we automate to remove labor from the process and to reduce the cycle time to give the customer faster response and reduce inventory costs. But these perceptions are not necessarily correct. The percentage of labor cost to total cost in most U.S. industries is low. The reduction of labor with the objective of reducing labor costs has very little leverage.

In a production line, the time that parts wait to be processed by the next machine or person is known as *queue time*. These parts are actually idle while waiting in line. In U.S. industry, this queue or idle time comprises 90 to 95 percent of the total manufacturing cycle.[5] This statistic is an astonishing example of inefficiency, yet with few exceptions, it is the norm for U.S. manufacturing. Unless the basic reasons for this excessive queue time are solved, speeding up the machines or moving parts faster between machines, whether achieved by automation or otherwise, will have a minimal effect on cycle time. Unless we attack the basic causes of the very high queue times, working on the 5 to 10 percent value add time will be of limited help.

Thus, if the replacement of labor to reduce labor costs and the reduction of cycle time are not valid reasons for automation of production, particularly in capital-intensive industries, then why automate at all? One reason is the need for process control. In many of the most important U.S. industries, the nature and complexity of the processes used in manufacturing these products demand repeatability, reliability, and high yield of product. Submicroscopic contaminants at one process step can render a product useless. What would normally be regarded as inconsequential human error can result in serious deterioration in product performance and quality. If the elimination of humans from production can improve the control of the process, reduce the amount of these contaminants, and eliminate human error, then the cost of automation is well worth the investment. Automation for this reason may result not only in reduced costs but a much better product. Furthermore, automation could make it feasible to manufacture products that couldn't be produced by manual techniques.

Has automation ever succeeded in the past? The record clearly shows that it has, and dramatically so. From the 1930s to 1960s major gains in productivity were made with the use of automation. Of course, automation during that era was far from the automation now envisioned for the future. During that era, automation consisted mostly of replacing labor-intensive operations with individual machines that performed each function with much less labor involvement. There was little or no automatic linkage between steps in the assembly line except for some mechanized conveyors moving parts from one station to another. There was little or no computer control, of course, because the computer was only in its infancy until the late 1950s. But to the extent that that process can be called automation, it was extremely successful. Whether we might expect the same dramatic advances with automation in the next ten or twenty years is another matter, though. Many changes that have occurred since that era, paradoxically due in part to the very success of automation itself, make the likelihood of similar success problematic.

First, automation has converted high labor-intensive industries to low labor- and high capital-intensive ones. Most of the smokestack industries, including automobiles, textiles, garments, and machinery, have experienced this change. As a consequence, much less labor content in these industries now can be replaced with automation.

Another factor that influences the future direction of automation is the dwindling market share for U.S. companies and the accompanying reduction in the utilization of manufacturing capacity. Very long queue times and poor equipment utilization (a U.S. average of 30 percent of equipment capacity)[6] contributed to high manufacturing costs. These increasing costs reduced demand for U.S. products and decreased U.S. market share. This lower demand further reduced capacity utilization creating further cost increases. A vicious cycle of lower demand and higher cost further reduced U.S. competitiveness in world markets.

Finally, there has been a strong shift from low technology industries (such as the so-called smokestack industries) to high technology (computers, semiconductors, telecommunications). These high technology industries are very capital-intensive and are highly volatile, unstable, and difficult to automate. For all of these reasons, the leverage of automation for cost reduction is lower than ever before.

This does not mean that automation will not play a part in the future of industry, but we must use it carefully and selectively, capitalizing on its strengths and avoiding its weaknesses and risks in a highly dynamic technological world.

There are two directions that factory automation could take in the future. One direction could be the totally automated production line, untouched by human hands. The other direction is a far more realistic one than the science fiction version of automation. It is an integrated system of people, processes, informaton systems, and tools. It integrates manual operations, mechanized processes, and computer control systems. People still render human judgments, and mechanized tools speed up the operations and carry out processes in a controlled and repeatable way. Computers keep track of the product and provide the mass of data necessary to control the production in an organized way. The advantages of automation and mechanization can be obtained while still retaining the needed flexibility to accommodate the demands of this volatile technological era. Most of all, automation will permit us to dramatically increase productivity by applying resources to the areas of greatest productivity leverage.

CA*RE*: The Role of Industrial Robots

The Robot Institute of America (RIA) defines an industrial robot as "a reprogrammable multifunctional manipulator designed to move material, parts, tools, or specialized devices, through variable programmed motions for the performance of a variety of tasks."[7] An industrial robot is a special machine that is basically a direct replacement for human labor. Most robots perform simple, repetitive, and unskilled tasks and perform these tasks in essentially the same manner and at the same speed that a person would perform them.

Industrial robots have been used worldwide for material handling, welding, spray painting, and assembly. The material handling robots include all applications in which the robot is picking up, transferring, or moving parts, including machine loading and unloading, tasks for equipment such as forming processes, removing parts from die casting machines, palletizing and depalletizing parts, and stacking and unstacking and packing and unpacking operations. Robots are used for spot welding and metal/inert gas welding. Spray painting robot applications are more complex and expensive and offer a possible solution in areas where chemicals would pose a health hazard to human beings.

Probably the area with the greatest potential for application of robots is assembly—processes in which parts are brought together, fitted, screwed in place, or, otherwise connected to each other. According to some estimates, 85 percent of all manual labor expended in industry in the United States could be classified as assembly.

Robots are often used for hot, tiring, difficult, dirty, unhealthy, and dangerous tasks. Their use often may be justified for maintaining high and consistent standards of quality and decreasing rejects and rework. In some applications, they may be used to improve appearance, consistency, and uniformity. Robots are even used for pickup and delivery of mail. In short, the most widely accepted justification for robots is for the replacement of direct labor for simple, repetitive, and unskilled tasks.

The principal and most obvious savings that would result from the use of industrial robots is the cost of the direct labor they replace. To understand this savings, consider the fact that for almost all U.S. industries direct labor is less than 20 percent of the total product cost (see chapter 3). Now consider that there were fewer than 10,000 robots in operation in the United States in 1983.[8] The total direct labor savings in the entire country can be computed for a range of labor rates that represent a wide spectrum of industries. We have assumed in the calculations shown in table 6–4 that operating costs including interest, programming, and maintenance for a typical industrial robot are approximately $5.00 per hour.[9] If these savings are compared with the total value of manufacturing of products in the United States each year (approximately $750 billion), they are virtually insignificant.

Does all this mean that the promise of industrial robotics has been oversold? The answer is not clear. That the use of robots solely to replace direct labor is of small, almost insignificant value in lowering manufacturing costs is supported by the facts. But as suggested earlier, there are many other reasons for replacing some direct labor with these devices. The achievement of consistent standards of quality, low reject rates, and faster throughput will become at least as important as the cost reduction resulting from the replacement of labor. Furthermore, as we move into the latter part of this century and into the next, the technology of robotics will certainly advance, making robots even more versatile. Their ultimate impact on industry and society is yet to be realized.

CARE: Electronics: The Foundation of Modern Industry

Electronics has revolutionized far more than the computer. It has permeated almost every industry and influenced practically every aspect of U.S. society. The application of electronics in industrial and consumer

Table 6–4
Estimate of Potential Annual U.S. Direct Labor Cost Savings Due to Robot Implementation in 1983
(millions of dollars)

Direct Labor Rate per Hour	Number of Direct Workers Replaced per Robot		
	1	2	3
$5	$ 0	$104	$208
$10	104	208	312
$20	312	624	936

Assumption: Forty-hour work week, fifty-two weeks per year.

products has been the area of greatest growth in the last two decades. The productivity impact of electronics has been felt in every aspect of our lives. The last twenty years can truly be characterized as the age of microelectronics.

Few innovations are more spectacular than the microprocessor. First microprocessors were applied to toys and games. Then they penetrated and eventually dominated consumer electronics in calculators, push-button telephones, television, audio and audiovisual equipment, watches, computer games, and many more products. Hardly a product in the marketplace is not being improved by the microprocessor—automobiles, television, home appliances, typewriters, copiers, sewing machines, and almost any type of entertainment equipment. It is difficult, in fact, to conceive of any product that will continue to be manufactured competitively without microprocessors.

In the factory, almost all equipment contains microprocessors. The role of microprocessors in robots and automation continues to expand. In business and industry the growth of software for the microcomputer has far exceeded that of the minicomputer and the mainframe computer.

All areas of software growth for the microprocessor, including sales, distribution, financial, accounting, word processing, filing, graphics, and systems software, have outpaced the minicomputer and the mainframe applications. According to the *New Scientist,* "the application market for microprocessing technology is about 38 percent of the world's present economy."[10]

The impact of electronics on communications has been almost as profound as its impact on computers. Electronics is the base for all modern communications media: telephone, telegraph, radio, television, and satellite. Electronic publishing, the newest form of communications, is turning the television screen into a constantly up-to-date source of information. The retrieval of information from on-line data bases using a special terminal or microcomputer and telephone line is already several decades old. But two new forms of electronic publishing are particularly exciting. Teletext is an electronic magazine that consists of up to thousands of pages or *frames* (video screens) of graphics and information distributed via cable or broadcast television signals. Teletext routinely carries timely information such as news, weather, sports, traffic conditions, and other local information.

Videotex, the more technically complex of the applications, employs a large control computer that can interact simultaneously with thousands of users. A videotext service is intended to be a graphically attractive home information retrieval service that replaces the original forms of text-only electronic publishing services.

Electronics are so widespread in U.S. society that before 1990 the electronics-based industry could approach a half trillion dollars, larger than any industry ever created.[11] Despite this pervasiveness, electronics has yet to have a competitive influence on overall U.S. industrial productivity.

What Has the Headlong Plunge into CARE Done for U.S. Productivity?

Electronics, automation, robotics, computers, and communications have definitely revolutionized our lives. The technological advances of the last twenty years have been awesome: virtually no aspect of U.S. society is not influenced strongly by them. They have given us games to have fun with, spellbinding science fiction movies, jet airplanes to speed us to our destinations, space vehicles to explore the cosmos, and communications equipment to contact our loved ones at the push of a few buttons. They help us with our banking, shopping, driving, and eating. They greatly assist medical science and lengthen our lives. These are all to the good.

But what have these great innovations done to industrial productivity, the U.S. standard of living, and the United States' economic health? Despite the excitement, glamour, and challenge of the four elements of CARE, the United States lags behind the major industrial powers of the world in productivity growth—behind not just Japan, but Italy, Germany, and the United Kingdom as well.

Has CARE been oversold? Do other factors degrade productivity more than CARE increases it? Should the United States abandon CARE and look for some other magic potion to cure U.S. productivity ills? CARE may have been oversold, but this doesn't mean that it isn't a good strategy. A headlong plunge into the world of CARE is not a cure-all in the pursuit of productivity. We believe that the correct identification of the major areas of productivity leverage, and the application of the productivity techniques in this book, will lead to major improvements in productivity. Then the judicious application of CARE in selected areas, using our techniques, will yield powerful results.

7
Believe It or Not, We're Counterproductive

Conventional Measurements That AIL Productivity

Managers of any enterprise—whether a bank, production line, restaurant, or football team—need a system of measurements. They must know at all times the condition of the business, its costs, and its results. They must know who is doing a good job, who is performing below expectations, where the problems are, and what to do about them. But measurements are valuable only if they are used to measure the right things. The wrong set of measurements may deceive us into believing that things are good when they are really bad, or bad when they are really good. They may even force us to make the wrong decision because the measurement is giving the wrong information. Moreover, some measurements may serve a business well for a long time but must be changed and modernized because of the changing state of the industry.

Labor and Other Commonly Used Productivity Measurements

For several decades the most basic and commonly used measure of productivity was *output per hour* or *output per direct labor hour*. If two hours are required to produce 1,000 parts, productivity is 500 parts per hour. If we require two people to work for one hour to produce 1,000 parts, productivity is 500 parts per direct labor hour. There has been such a preoccupation with the use of direct labor hour as the productivity measurement that it might be concluded that the only way to improve productivity is to improve the efficiency of the direct worker.

There are several reasons why labor has been by far the most popular factor used in measuring productivity. The first and most obvious reason is that in the past direct labor constituted a much larger percentage of the total cost of producing goods than it does today. Controlling labor and improving its efficiency obviously had a great deal of leverage in the improvement of productivity. A second reason is that measuring the performance and efficiency of labor is simpler than measuring other elements of production. It is much easier to measure the efficiency of a keypunch operator, bank teller, or assembly-line worker than it is to measure the efficiency of a chief executive officer, engineer, bank president, or production control manager.

A third reason is that productivity has become an important subject in wage negotiations between labor and management. In these negotiations, wage agreements are linked to productivity. The labor unions desire to ensure that improvements in labor productivity are coupled with improved wages and working conditions. Management has the same desire for linking wages and productivity; it wants to achieve improvements in productivity to offset the costs of higher paychecks for labor.

The use of the measurement of output per direct labor hour has at least three shortcomings, however:

1. Production operations of any industry consist of many elements, of which labor is only one. Output per man-hour does not measure the productive efficiency of the whole operation; in fact, it does not even measure the productive contribution of labor itself.
2. Increases in output per man-hour may be desirable, but in many cases such increases are actually not desirable. These increases may not even reduce unit labor costs, particularly where bottlenecks exist elsewhere in the manufacturing process.
3. Even if increases in output per man-hour are accompanied by a proportionate increase in hourly wage rates, production costs are more likely to increase than remain unchanged in capital-dominated industries.

Because labor content is decreasing as a percentage of the total cost of a product and because the emphasis on measuring labor efficiency should therefore be changed do not mean that labor itself is becoming less important. On the contrary, labor continues to be possibly the most important component of both manufacturing and nonmanufacturing operations. But labor is a partner in a total system that includes management, materials, machines, engineers, and maintenance personnel, and its effectiveness must be measured as a part of the whole system. Because of the interactions among all of these parts of the system, measuring the efficiency of one of the parts, such as direct labor, has quite limited significance in measuring productivity.

Many factors can contribute to productivity, and efforts have been made to define and improve its measurement. One definition of productivity is the ratio of total output to total input or the ratio of the results achieved to the resources consumed. Another definition is the ratio of the effectiveness with which organization goals are achieved to the efficiency with which resources are consumed in the course of these achievements. These measurements are all attempts to recognize that many factors contribute to productivity. These methods can be effective in assessing the total productivity of an operation. They can measure the collective efficiency of all of the factors that in combination, translate resources into production of goods or services. The disadvantage in such measurements is that they cannot differentiate among the individual contributors to the total productivity.

In chapter 6, we discussed the four factors of CARE (computers, automation, robotics, electronics) and how their inappropriate use can actually limit productivity even though they were intended to dramatically improve it. There are other reasons for the United States' ailing productivity record. Three areas of measurements are commonly used to improve productivity, but if these measurements are used in the wrong way, as they often are, the results can have a negative effect. Instead of improving productivity, they can seriously limit or even reduce it. These three areas are

A̲ccounting efficiencies

I̲ndustrial engineering standards

L̲abor ratios

It is no coincidence that this acronym, AIL, accurately describes the illness caused by inappropriate use of these three measurements.

Accounting Efficiencies[1]

One doesn't have to be a cost accountant to recognize that cost accounting is essential. Many cost accounting controls and practices have brought order out of chaos and have resulted in enormous increases in profit, productivity, and efficiency. But times are changing and cost accounting methods must change to keep up. The misapplication of cost accounting techniques is far more widespread than is commonly believed, and their misuse can seriously hamper the very objectives they are supposed to serve—increased productivity and reduced product cost.

Several common cost accounting practices are outdated and often misapplied. Most of the Fortune 500 companies use a standard cost accounting system that allocates all nondirect costs on the basis of direct labor hours. This method of allocating nondirect costs was acceptable in the past, as long as the majority of the cost of product was direct labor. The following hypothetical decisions are based on actual standard cost accounting practices.

Multinat, a multinational company, was manufacturing two major categories of products at one of its largest locations. The first was old standard products, and the other new leading-edge products. One-third of the direct labor hours were used to manufacture the old standard products. The equipment required to fabricate the standard product was completely written off. The out-of-pocket cost to manufacture the standard products was virtually negligible and consisted of direct labor and materials. However, because standard products used one-third the direct labor in the entire factory, they were allocated exactly one-third of the capital and overhead cost. This made the production of standard products look prohibitively expensive—even though the actual out-of-pocket costs were minuscule. On paper, it was far cheaper to buy these products from a supplier who was not in the business of manufacturing new products and, as a result, did not have high capital and overhead costs. The supplier was charging Multinat in excess of five times the out-of-pocket cost of Multinat. Yet the supplier appeared a more attractive financial proposition simply because the method of allocating capital and overhead costs was based on the proportion of direct labor used.

In another situation, the Innovate Corporation attempted to introduce a leading-edge advanced product using a revolutionary process. This product required considerable direct labor because of the excessive rework and inspection necessary for the early stages of manufacturing. Due to the relatively high direct-labor content, a large proportion of the capital and overhead costs of the entire factory were allocated to this product. This made the advanced product look very expensive, even though the actual out-of-pocket capital and overhead investment was much lower than what was being allocated. Because of this misallocation of costs, the production of the leading-edge product was terminated and a very lucrative and competitive opportunity was lost.

These examples illustrate how foolish "make" versus "buy" decisions and investment decisions are made based on outmoded standard cost accounting practices.

Another misuse of cost accounting practices relates to the use of *standard costs*. Industrial engineering develops standard costs based on production standards. The *earned standard cost* is determined by multiplying the actual production by the standard cost. By comparing the *earned standard cost* to *actual payroll costs*, management can measure the efficiency of an operation.

When these calculations are completed, what do we do with them? We presumably use them to measure the performance of each department. But the achievement of "success" so measured does not ensure productivity or real efficiency. Understandably, the department manager wants the highest efficiency rating. Even if the department performing the next production processes is a bottleneck, the ambitious department manager still concentrates on preserving his manpower and getting a high grade, perhaps unnecessarily consuming raw materials and building up a costly work-in-process inventory. Operating expenses increase, but throughput doesn't, and the high efficiency rating of this department manager contributes nothing to productivity, cost, throughput, or profit.

Industrial Engineering Standards

Industrial engineers have played a major role in the improvement of productivity in industry. But this field, too, must become sensitive to changes in the business environment. Classical industrial engineering is based on techniques such as methods engineering, time study standards and measurements, establishment of wage incentive programs, and standard costs. Industrial engineers concentrate on work simplification, use of flow process charts, method improvement, operations analysis, motion economy, man and machine charts, work sampling, time study standards, and wage incentives based on standard man-hours or earned dollars. Most of these techniques still continue to concentrate on direct labor.

Because the portion of product cost that is attributable to labor is shrinking, why do we give so much attention to it? There is a lack of realization that labor is not only shrinking but is already only a small fraction of the total product cost. Sometimes U.S. industry acts like a doctor who concentrates the physical examination of an accident victim on one toe while neglecting the rest of the body.

This preoccupation with direct labor, whether it is assembling parts on a manufacturing line or processing paper in a bank, is not the only menace to productivity. The greater danger is the use of outmoded standards such as pieces per hour, pieces per shift, or man-hours per 100 pieces applied to determine production efficiencies. Stated in terms of a formula,

$$\text{Production efficiency} = \frac{\text{Total earned man-hours}}{\text{Actual hours worked}}$$

Measuring efficiency is not a problem, if efficiency is measured correctly and meaningfully. Most companies measure the performance of their workers individually or on a department basis. This has the advantage of helping appraise individual and management performance. The problem with a measurement on this basis is that many employees may earn superior marks, but overall productivity may actually suffer. Employees want to do their best and get the highest appraisals. Department heads want to keep their workers busy and show the best performance for their departments. This is comparable to a basketball team where everyone concentrates on scoring the most baskets. Even if all of the players are superstars, lack of teamwork usually will result in defeat. Similarly, an orchestra of virtuosos can sound like mush if the members play like soloists and not an ensemble.

Consider a series of successive operations in a factory. A separate department performs each operation, and department heads desire to keep their people busy and productive. But department 2 is a bottleneck; it needs additional labor to break the bottleneck. Department 1 has plenty of work and is trying with great success to keep very busy and achieve good results. It consumes raw materials, meets all of its measurements, accumulates an inventory of parts, and passes this inventory to department 2. The inventory sits in department 2 for long periods of time because it is a bottleneck and can't get the parts out. The manager and employees of department 1 are awarded prizes, a free lunch, and a very high appraisal. But their excellent individual performance has served no purpose. Inventory and operating expenses increased while the output of the line decreased. The triumphant department head certainly wouldn't volunteer to move machines and people to the ailing department. He was being measured by his performance, no one else's. This is a common example of a measurement that actually harms productivity. In other words, the many processes and operations used to build a product are not beads on a string to be observed and measured one at a time. They are, in fact, pieces of an intricate mosaic, all of whose pieces touch on and affect all other pieces.

In addition to free lunches and good appraisals, wage incentive programs are often used to reward good performance. When properly applied, these programs have been directly responsible for impressive productivity gains. But improperly used, they can have the opposite effect that management intends. If people are paid extra money for individual or department level accomplishments, they are given an added incentive to excel at the department or individual level, regardless of what they are doing to assist in the overall productivity of the total organization. What employee can resist the temptation to earn more money? What department head will sacrifice more pay for himself and employees in order to assist other departments in improving their performance so that overall productivity of the line will increase? In the proper management environment and with good team players, these sacrifices will be made.

But paying people for higher individual or department efficiency makes such teamwork much more difficult. These wage incentive programs are paying people for performance that may actually increase costs.

An incentive system known as the Scanlan plan attempts to solve this problem. All members associated with a manufacturing operation—management, direct labor, engineering—have a monetary interest in the overall productivity of the factory. All people associated with making the enterprise work—engineers, direct labor, maintenance—are mobilized for the purpose of moving the needed resources to bottleneck areas to solve critical problems. In other words, people are rewarded monetarily for a successful total enterprise. A rigid measurement system that rewards individuals or small independent groups prevents flexibility. Incentive plans have their place but must be applied with great discretion.

Japanese industry has become adept at identifying and eliminating production bottlenecks with KANBAN, just-in-time, and JIDOKA systems. It has accomplished this by exercising great flexibility in quickly deploying people and tools to bottleneck areas where there are manpower shortages.

It may be shocking to realize, but industrial engineers often spend too much time cutting costs. After all, isn't cost-cutting the main reason for improving productivity and increasing competitiveness? Of course we want to cut costs, but it is far more important to increase revenue and profit. If we try to nibble away at different elements of cost, we may nibble at the wrong elements. Management has a normal inclination to urge industrial engineers to cut the cost of all elements of the total cost of a product. It believes that if labor, capital, materials, and burden are reduced, the total cost will be reduced. As is discussed in a later chapter, these actions may actually be counterproductive. Cutting resources to cut costs may drastically reduce ability to produce more product and increase revenue and profitability. Cutting resources may result in some short-term improvements, not only in production costs but also in the bottom line for this year. But its long-term consequences can be disastrous for any business that wants to stay in business.

Direct Labor Ratio

At the beginning of the Industrial Revolution and well into the twentieth century, industry was very labor intensive. The performance of these industries—their productivity, output, and costs—directly depended on the performance of manual labor. The need to achieve greater efficiency from its labor was an understandable preoccupation of management.

Dramatic gains in smokestack industries such as automobiles, steel, textiles, railroads, machinery, appliances, garments, and shoes would never have been possible without management's emphasis on increasing the performance of and decreasing the amount of direct labor. In fact, the major strides in mass production that were achieved during the last several decades would never have been taken without a systematic approach to the reduction of direct labor.

As a result of these strides in labor efficiency, and as a result of mechanization, the labor content of most U.S. industries has dramatically decreased. Today, much of U.S. industry has been converted to capital intensiveness with a low content of direct labor. For a large part of U.S. industry, labor content has decreased to 10 percent or less of the cost of manufacturing; it is seldom greater than 20 percent. The leverage in further reducing direct labor is itself becoming smaller.

Since the labor content of industry has been so drastically reduced, preoccupation with carefully monitoring and attempting to reduce labor can have exactly the opposite effect that it is intended to have. Capital-intensive industries are frequently at the leading edge of technology and experience a high rate of change. These industries have also experienced a precipitous growth. Because they have not been able to consistently keep up with escalating demand, they are often constrained in production capacity. In this environment, their problem has not been a costly excess of direct labor, but rather a shortage of labor in certain critical operations that have limited their capacity.

A common measurement used in U.S. industry is the ratio of indirect labor to direct labor. If a plant historically has run with a ratio of 2 indirects to 1 direct, financial and manufacturing management assume that every time one direct worker is hired, two indirects automatically arrive at the door at the same time. A major way that they can control indirect growth is to limit additions of directs.

Furthermore, managers have been conditioned for decades to carefully control direct labor, and any suggestion of an increase is subjected to intense scrutiny. After all, they argue, if the operating departments would do their job, the increases would be unnecessary. *Unnecessary* is, however, very difficult to define, particularly in a complex new product or technology. Additional direct labor may be unnecessary in following the manufacturing plan, but the plan is seldom correct. The savings in controlling the labor level may be wiped out many times by the loss in output and increase in cycle time and inventory caused by severe bottlenecks. Therefore, preoccupation with controlling direct labor out of fear that both direct and indirect labor costs will skyrocket can be dangerously exaggerated. As will be shown in chapter 8, the addition of small amounts of direct labor in critical areas of almost any business can have a profound impact on productivity.

A second ratio, capital to direct labor, is also subject to much abuse and misunderstanding. Executives often have a preconceived idea of what this ratio should be, a belief that often is influenced by the way their company has operated over a long period of time. By adhering to this ratio, they feel that everything is under control. The problem with this approach is that about the only factor they really are controlling is the ratio itself. Everything else could go out of control by using this irrelevant measurement. The actual level of capital per direct labor must change with the products and technologies. Capital will change with time as products undergo a period of learning and as new tools are introduced into production. The actual ratio of capital to direct labor increases as industries become increasingly capital-intensive. If this ratio is enforced blindly, a small percentage increase in direct labor could lead to a very high and unnecessary capital expenditure. It would be a case of the tail wagging the dog. There is no magic ratio. Instead of controlling the operations, this type of measurement can put it in a strait jacket. There may be some merit in its use for comparison purposes with other companies making the same products or performing the same service. But using it for control and decision making can be very dangerous. Any ratios comparing capital, indirects, materials, or overhead to direct labor should be used with great caution. They are simplistic; they can create more problems than they solve.

A Measurement System for Productivity Leadership

Americans are more prone to follow fads than are people of most other nations. A fad is "a practice or interest followed for a time with exaggerated zeal."[2] Diets, hoola hoops, pet rocks, and more recently Cabbage Patch dolls are but a few examples of this tendency. The rush to use the four elements of CARE (see chapter 6)—computers, automation, robotics, and electronics—for the purpose of increasing productivity has some of the characteristics of faddism. Of course, such frivolous fads as pet rocks and hoola hoops are of short duration and have relatively little utility. CARE is revolutionary and will have enormous influence over society. Although CARE has often been misapplied and its power to increase U.S. productivity has so far been limited, it can and will ultimately have a much greater productivity image if we know how to apply it properly.

The three elements of AIL discussed in this chapter cannot be characterized as a fad. They have been used with great success for many decades. They are firmly embedded in the U.S. industrial psyche. But they have become outmoded and are seriously limiting U.S. productivity.

If AIL is no longer a viable system for leadership, then what is? Before a useful system can be developed, we must first determine the goals of industry. There is certainly one goal on which every business person can agree: the major goal of every business—whether large manufacturing company, bank, corner grocery store, or restaurant—is to make money, to earn a profit. Of course, as *In Search of Excellence*[3] and other books have shown, any business must serve its customers well, sell a competitively priced and high-quality product, be a responsible citizen in the community, and provide the best possible environment for its employees. But none of these goals can be accomplished unless the business makes a profit. Any effective measurement system must be oriented toward that goal.

Notwithstanding our criticisms of some popular techniques of evaluating performance and productivity, many widely used measurements give a very good view of the overall health of any business. For example, the *return on investment* (ROI) is an excellent financial measure of the bottom-line operating performance of any profit-oriented organization. Variations of this indicator are *rate of return on total assets* (ROTA) and the *rate of profit on investment* (RPI). The rate of return on total assets is a ratio of net operating income (before interest expense and income taxes) to average assets available. The rate of profit on investment is simply profit divided by total investment.

Gross and *net profit* are also essential measurements for any business. Gross profit is the money received for products and services minus the total costs. Net profit is even more important because it is the real measure of how much money is made by the business and how much money remains after all expenses and taxes are paid.

The purpose of any profit-oriented organization is to increase all these financial measurements. But even though such indicators successfully serve this purpose, they are not necessarily good measures of productivity. A company that shows constant improvements in these indicators can justifiably claim that its productivity may be improving. But these measurements don't tell the management *why* productivity is improving, nor do they show managers *where* to look for the reasons and solutions to problems if the measurements do not improve.

In order to manage a business, managers need more than an overall assessment of success or failure. They must continuously identify specific problems and find their solutions. They need to define measurements that will give detailed indicators of how the business is working so that they can manage it instead of being managed by it.

In addition to the goals we have described as pertinent to all business endeavors, five particular goals are the underpinning of any production operation:

↑ Throughput

↓ Inventory

↓ Operating expense

↓ Cycle time

↑ Yield

The arrows point to the direction that we want each goal to take. The basic objectives are the increase of throughput and yield and the decrease of inventory, cycle time, and operating expense. To increase productivity, these factors must be measured; their measurement will serve as the bases for decisions that management must make to increase productivity and profit.

In later chapters, including several case studies, we show how these five goals and measurements were made the basis for decisions that have resulted in major productivity improvements.

For the purposes of this book, these goals can be defined as follows:

Throughput: a measure of the rate of output or production. It is the volume of goods produced for a given time period (such as pieces per day).

Inventory: a measure of the parts and materials that are purchased and converted in various states of completion. It represents the money invested in partially or fully completed goods.

Operating expense: a measure of the money spent to achieve a level of output.

Cycle time: the total time required to manufacture a product. It consists of two components—idle or queue time and value add or work time.

Yield: the ratio of the number of good units completed divided by the maximum possible number available at an operation. Yield, usually expressed as a percentage, is relevant mostly to high technology manufacturing where yields are often very low (0 to 10 percent) during the early life of a product.

Part II
The Productivity
Techniques

8
Increasing the Output

The Importance of Bottlenecks

Unbalanced production lines are not very productive. Even ancient civilizations probably used some rudimentary forms of line balancing to speed up production or construction processes. While it is rare for today's managers of plants, grocery stores, or banks to admit that their enterprises are unbalanced, unbalanced lines nevertheless remain one of the most formidable barriers to high productivity.

In order to understand line balancing and recognize its complexity, a review of the concept of the bottleneck is required. A manufacturing bottleneck is a section of the line that restricts the amount of product that the line can produce. A line is unbalanced if it has one or more bottlenecks. More than any other production problem, the bottleneck is a phenomenon closely related to the obstacles that we all face in our daily lives. Long waits at the tollbooth while the minutes tick off until the time of an imminent plane departure, interminable delays at the bank, long lines at the grocery checkout counter are all due to the bottleneck problem.

These problems are frustrating, and their solutions may not always be easy. Planning the traffic on roads and the service at stores and banks is complicated by the fact that the demand for these services varies with the day of the week, season of the year, weather, and even economic conditions. Of course, well-planned banks and stores can anticipate many of these fluctuating conditions and prevent, or at least minimize, some of these inconveniences to their customers. Indeed, businesses have a great stake in solving these problems. Not only do bottlenecks result in problems and frustrations for the customer, but they also may cause serious productivity and cost problems for the business enterprise. It can be very costly to tie up valuable space, equipment, and employees' time while customers stand in line unattended. If this type of problem is multiplied countless times throughout the country, the result to the national economy and corporate profitability can be serious.

Perhaps more tollbooths, banktellers, and checkout counters could alleviate some of these problems, but why talk about bottlenecks in a productivity book if the solutions are so obvious? Unfortunately the solutions are neither simple nor obvious. The price paid for major imbalances in production lines and service activities, as well as for the giant bottlenecks that create these imbalances, is extremely high. These imbalances constitute one of the major barriers to high productivity. These problems are increasingly difficult to solve but must be understood to give the competitive edge to U.S. industries to increase our standard of living, remain competitive in the world, and promote economic growth.

Many sophisticated industrial engineering and operations research techniques have been developed to improve productivity and throughput (output) of manufacturing lines. But few, if any, of these techniques help managers identify production bottlenecks in an objective and quantitative manner. A method that can distinguish between chronic bottlenecks and those that are sporadic should result in a permanent improvement of the productivity and throughput of the line.

The normal methods of increasing productivity in a constrained factory involve a series of tactical moves that result in immediate but temporary results. These methods include an emphasis on working harder, overtime, use of weekends and additional shifts, and allocation of the most skilled workers to expedite products through the production line.

Another method is to bring together management representatives from the major production organizations including manufacturing, production control, manufacturing engineering, industrial engineering, maintenance, and quality control. Although this kind of meeting is supposed to be a forum in which to exchange ideas on how to increase production, it often instigates a great deal of finger-pointing and mutual criticism. Production control is blamed for poor planning and scheduling, manufacturing for inept labor performance and inefficient expediting. Equipment engineering is castigated for inferior equipment design and low availability and serviceability. Quality control is accused of writing unnecessarily tight specifications. Maintenance is blamed for taking too long to make repairs. Although this exercise may have some psychological value, these meetings seldom result in a solution to problems.

In addition, the tendency in U.S. industry is for management to concentrate on solutions to short-term problems. Certainly short-term action is necessary in any industry, usually to keep the production line flowing to supply the marketplace. But these short-term actions, however necessary, often are analogous to medical emergency treatment: after a serious accident, a tourniquet may be required immediately to stop the flow of blood from a broken artery to keep the injured person alive, but a much more fundamental course of action needs to be taken to cure the patient.

In a typical production line, steps can be taken to correct emergency situations. A normal response to the appearance of a bottleneck is to direct extra resources where excessive inventory exists. When additional production is called for, the production manager increases releases of parts into the line. This causes a large amount of excess inventory, a *work-in-process (WIP) bubble* at the beginning of the line. Overtime, additional shifts, weekends, temporary direct labor are used to move this WIP bubble to the next operation. As this bubble travels down the line, the extra manpower follows it. Although this technique of moving the WIP bubble through the production line will result in an immediate increase in production, it does not increase productivity, nor does it permanently solve the problem of production shortages. To achieve long-term improvement in productivity and lasting increase in production levels, fundamental changes must occur in the methods by which the manufacturing line is managed.

Bottlenecks: How Do We Find Them?

A simple but fundamental principle for eliminating bottlenecks is presented in the methods of line balancing discussed in this book. Unless the output of the section of the line that has the lowest output level is increased, there is little value in taking actions to increase the output of those sectors that are already producing at a higher level. There is no value in improving or widening a four-lane highway intersecting a bridge with one tollbooth. This tollbooth is clearly a chronic bottleneck: unless the bottleneck is solved, the flow of traffic will continue to be severely limited. Anyone who has driven during the rush hour over the George Washington Bridge in New York City or through the Callahan Tunnel in Boston has experienced this problem.

As production lines become increasingly complicated, it becomes more and more difficult to locate the chronic bottlenecks. The key to line balancing is to find a technique that will help managers locate the chronic bottlenecks, understand why they exist, determine how to eliminate them, and finally take the necessary action to eliminate them.

To analyze the capability of a manufacturing line, first divide it into measurable entities or sections, referred to in this book as *sectors*. A sector comprises a group of manufacturing operations that generally serves a manufacturing function. Commonly known sectors in the semiconductor industry are process steps such as oxidation, diffusion, lithography, metal evaporation, and quartz sputtering. For example, the lithography sector consists of photoresist application, baking, optical exposure, developing, and visual inspection operations.

Next, the performance of this particular line and of each sector must be characterized in some quantitative way so that the line's behavior is known precisely. One method for doing this is to use a product-tracking logistics system to measure and analyze performance. In such a system, the product is tracked on both entering and leaving each sector. With the line grouped in this manner, and with the aid of a tracking system, it is possible to develop a technique for identifying chronic bottlenecks.

First, the performance of each sector must be measured. The most meaningful and common measurements of a production line are *through-put* or *production rate, work-in-process inventory,* and *cycle time.* In order to plan production levels, the expected number of parts to be started and completed each day must be estimated. Furthermore, a plan must be far more precise than that. To ensure that the total output rate can be achieved, the plan also must include an expected rate of production at every sector, the expected level of work-in-process inventory before each sector, and the cycle time. There is nothing unusual or novel about such planning. Every line is normally planned with traditional industrial engineering methods that calculate these factors considering the performance of the labor and the number of machines to be used in the line. But as was stated earlier, these factors are merely assumptions: they are often wrong and do not represent a realistic description of the line performance.

A true description of the line performance can be obtained only by measuring the actual performance against the plan. By comparing the actual throughput, work-in-process inventory, and cycle time with the planned performance at each sector, an accurate and objective representation of the line performance can be obtained.

Now that this performance has been measured, how do managers interpret it? What can manufacturing managers do when they first note that they are not achieving their plans? The most normal reaction, or overreaction, to the first indication of a problem is to take short-term emergency action to find a solution. Yet this may be the wrong thing to do. The value of monitoring the performance in this way is in the ability to identify chronic bottlenecks. There is little value in measuring these indicators only on a daily or weekly basis; some daily or weekly fluctuations may have little or no long-term significance. Just as the pulse of a human being is monitored as an indicator of health, so must the health of a production line be monitored. An occasional variation from the normal heartbeat in a human being may not indicate a problem, and short-term variations in the pulse of the line are normal and should be treated as such. It is the longer-term indicator of chronic illness that must be observed. To really locate chronic bottlenecks, these comparisons of planned to actual performance should be studied continuously, and at least six weeks should elapse before management concludes that a chronic bottleneck exists.

These measurements can help managers determine the health of the production line. Simply stated, *any sector that is operating at a through-put level considerably lower than plan and is accompanied by a work-in-process inventory level considerably greater than plan is a bottleneck.* Such a condition means that a sufficient level of inventory is present in the sector, assuming that a reasonable cycle time has been planned for that sector. It means that, for some reason, the manpower and machines that operate the sector cannot process the planned level of work even though sufficient parts exist with which to carry out that process. This condition represents a chronic bottleneck if it persists for an extended period.

The manufacturing line outlined in table 8–1 (the data for which is typical of numerous constrained manufacturing lines) is a simple example useful for identifying chronic bottlenecks. Even though the data shown represents a four-week period, it is necessary to track sector performance for a longer time in order to identify chronic bottlenecks.

Analysis of the line performance data in table 8–1 will result in the identification of sector 1 and sector 3 as chronic bottlenecks, and sector 4 as low throughput and low WIP (week 2 and week 3). Note that even though sector 4 has a consistently low throughput, it is not necessarily a chronic bottleneck because there is not enough work (WIP) in week 2 and week 3 to be processed. Sector 5 has a chronic condition of high WIP. Even though this sector cannot be classified as a bottleneck, management should take steps to reduce these excessive inventory levels.

Chronic Bottlenecks: How Do We Eliminate Them?

Chronic bottlenecks are major deterrents to high productivity; the cost of perpetuating them is enormous. But despite the difficulty in removing them, the benefits are tremendous. First, it is important to recognize that identification of the chronic bottlenecks is a major step in itself. The lack

Table 8–1
Sample Manufacturing Line

Sector	Cycle Time (Days)	Plan		Week 1		Week 2		Week 3		Week 4	
		ATR[a]	WIP[b]	ATR	WIP	ATR	WIP	ATR	WIP	ATR	WIP
1	1	400	400	250	600	275	800	300	1,000	250	1,250
2	3	390	1,170	400	950	375	1,000	420	850	375	990
3	2	380	760	225	900	250	1,500	240	2,300	275	3,000
4	1	370	370	250	370	225	200	250	100	240	350
5	2	360	720	360	1,500	370	1,400	380	1,300	390	1,200

[a]ATR is the average throughput rate.
[b]WIP is the average work-in-process inventory.

of such identification often creates confusion concerning what problems exist on the production line. It leads to ineffective management actions that offer no fundamental solution to the problems. The identification of chronic bottleneck sectors in a measurable, quantifiable, and noncontroversial manner is a prerequisite to their solution.

Once a chronic bottleneck has been identified by noncontroversial data, there is no need for further debate about the problem or who is to blame for the existence of the problem. What is essential, however, is that the bottleneck be eliminated so that long-term gains in production levels can be achieved.

One of the most frequent and powerful solutions to a production bottleneck is the infusion of the most skilled labor available into that sector. The combination of additional manpower and the high skill of that manpower can lead to almost an immediate, substantial—even dramatic—increase in throughput. Chapter 3 discussed the relatively low percentage of labor costs in a capital-intensive industry. Because of these low labor costs, dramatic production increases can be achieved with a very small increase in resources. If labor constitutes only a small percentage, on the order of 4 to 20 percent, of the total manufacturing cost, using a few additional direct labor people will have practically no influence on the total cost. Yet eliminating large chronic bottlenecks can increase the product output by as much as 50 to 100 percent. Such an increase resulting from the addition of so small a labor cost component constitutes a major increase in productivity. In actual practice on many production lines, great increases in productivity have been achieved by the strategic addition of manpower into chronic bottlenecks.

If such a simple step can result in such a phenomenal improvement in productivity, why isn't it adopted? The answers lie in some perceptions of how costs can be controlled in this type of manufacturing. First, most managers do not understand that chronic bottlenecks severely limit production in a constrained factory. Second, once the importance of such chronic bottlenecks is recognized, no simple method exists for characterizing the performance of the line in a quantitative manner so that the bottlenecks can be identified. Next, management often does not recognize the relatively low labor content of the total manufacturing cost.

Finally, financial management usually concentrates on labor costs because the financial, accounting, and productivity systems use direct labor costs as a prime basis for measurement and comparison. It is standard practice to relate direct labor to the amount of indirect manpower and overhead through what is often called the indirect-to-direct labor ratio. As has been shown, if a given ratio, for example 3 to 1, becomes acceptable, management fears that increasing the direct labor will automatically increase the indirect costs. Consequently, management becomes preoccupied with the control of direct labor costs. Furthermore, management is concerned about hiring more direct labor to meet increasing demand but having an excess of labor in a period of falling demand.

These are all legitimate concerns and must be seriously considered. But when decisions on the desirability of reducing, maintaining, or increasing the labor force are made, the enormous leverage that small increases in direct labor can have on output and productivity must become a prime consideration.

The problem of bottlenecks can be solved by many means other than adding direct labor. The appropriate solution depends on the nature of the bottleneck and the reasons for its existence. A new and complex piece of machinery may, for example, have a low utilization factor. A highly skilled maintenance team should be assigned to work with the tool on a long-term basis until the basic problems of low utilization are solved. Similarly, a troublesome new process that is difficult to control may require much greater attention from a skilled manufacturing engineer who is being moved from a more routine and less important project. Or a tool that is operating below its rated speed or capability may have to be supplemented with another tool until the performance is increased.

Initially, many managers demand the immediate solution of these tooling and process problems. They tolerate no excuses, spend a considerable time finding the offending organization, and assign blame. They direct lower levels of management to plan programs to bring about quick solutions. This results in charts that present long and impressive lists of action items in several colors. Even though many of these items will not be pursued, and others will take a long time to materialize, management assumes that the solutions to these problems are well on the way and moves on to other managerial problems. In the meantime, production continues to limp along at a disastrously low rate, and none of the fundamental problems responsible for this poor performance has been solved.

Of course, these tooling and process problems must eventually be solved, and management must insist that engineers plan for and pursue the necessary programs to solve them. But it would be a mistake to expect quick solutions to problems complicated as much by external as internal factors. In an era of high technology and constant advances in the state-of-the-art of manufacturing, a learning period for new processes and tools is inevitable. There is no simple way to accelerate progress. While the necessary engineering must be carried out to "learn" the manufacturing processes, management must recognize that it ignores major opportunities to increase production and productivity if it does not take the necessary steps that can yield major benefits. A long and methodical learning process is fundamental to all new advanced technologies. The opportunities lie in recognizing that solutions can be found to bottlenecks of the type described in this book and can result in major productivity improvement.

9
Streamlining the Operation

Cycle Time and Inventory: How to Reduce Them

The time required to manufacture a product is its *cycle time*. The length of this time is measured from the moment an order is released to the line until the product is completed. One of the most important objectives of any manufacturer is to reduce this cycle time to the lowest possible level. The manufacturer wastes money if costly delays occur in the manufacturing process. The costs of maintaining a high in-process inventory erode profitability and competitiveness. Delays in expediting the product result in delays in shipping the product to the customer. The buyer who must wait for three months before delivery of a much-needed product may well turn to a competitor who promises a one-month delivery of a similar product. In some industries, incomplete products languishing in the production line for extended periods of time may actually deteriorate in quality and performance before a final sealing or packaging process is carried out. All of these reasons make short cycle time a critical concern for managers.

The cycle time of any job has two components—idle or queue time and value add or work time. *Value add time* or *work time in production* is defined as the amount of time needed to actually perform the work. *Queue time* is defined as the remainder of the time that the job spends in the manufacturing line waiting in queues, generally at process centers or work stations. A casual analysis of cycle time will reveal that queue time is always larger than the work time, even for an efficiently run manufacturing line. A simple analogy to the problem of planning for cycle time is the rush to the airport to take a plane. Consider the time it takes to drive to the airport, park the car in the parking lot, check the luggage, get a seat assignment, buy a newspaper, pass through security, and race to the boarding gate: the traveler may arrive to discover the plane well on the way to its destination if no allowance is made for the delays that accompany each of these steps. True, each of these transactions might, in the best of all worlds, be carried out in a matter of minutes. But more likely there may be an extensive wait in a long line at each of these points. These queues usually take a considerably longer time than the specific transactions. Indeed, as frequent passengers of shuttle flights will confirm, the time expended in all these preparatory activities often exceeds the duration of the flight itself. The same situation exists in a production line, but with dire consequences if this problem is allowed to get out of control.

Like the journey to the airport boarding gate, when most of the time is spent waiting in lines for service, the manufacturing parts are waiting in line to be processed. Industry has placed great stress on improving the efficiency of labor and the productivity of machines to reduce cost by moving the product more rapidly through the production process. Yet in most manufacturing lines, the product spends 90 to 95 percent of the cycle time in queues. Even the most efficiently run manufacturing lines have queue times ranging between 60 to 70 percent of the total cycle time, and this kind of performance has rarely been sustained for more than a few months at a time. If this performance record is typical of U.S. industry, it is not surprising that efforts to improve overall productivity have not yielded very dramatic results. The effort to improve labor and machine productivity are important. But the opportunities to achieve major advances by improving cycle time are even greater.

Traditionally, manufacturing management devotes a great amount of attention to reducing the value add time. This time period is influenced by the equipment that performs a given process, the design of the product, and the process required to build it. In many industries, particularly high technology ones, the design of the equipment, the process, and the product are strongly interrelated. A small change in any one of these three elements can greatly influence the other two. Because of this, improving the productivity of a given operation is extremely complex. Management often attempts to increase the productivity of each step of the line by simplifying the process and changing the equipment design for greater speed, higher throughput, and reduced down-time. These objectives are often realistic and worthwhile and must be a part of any manufacturer's program to increase productivity. But equal and even greater attention must be given to the reduction of 90 percent or more of the time that the parts spend in the line. Unless this cycle time is reduced, efforts to decrease value add time will have limited results in overall productivity.

The Queue: What Causes It?

Two areas influence queue time: how the line is planned and how it is run. The plan is determined by the way the production capacity of the line is computed. These calculations are based on the type of product being made, the tools, processes, and materials used to make the product, and the many assumptions that must be made about the state of the technology and the mix of the different products. If we are making one size of paper clips or rubber bands, these problems are relatively easy. If we are making hundreds of different variations of a high technology product, the problems are immensely complex and planning for production is difficult and unpredictable. The influence of the running of the line is determined by the way jobs are scheduled, tracked, moved, and prioritized. These factors are discussed later in this section.

Before it is possible to obtain long-term reductions in queue times, management must first understand the basic reason for their existence. The first and most important reason deals with the learning process involved when any new product or technology is introduced. Like a baby's process of learning to walk, talk, eat, and read, a new technology must go through an extensive learning period of its own. When a new technology is first publicized in the press and the Nobel prizes are awarded for its invention, many years, possibly decades, pass before this technological innovation is used widely. The transistor was invented in the late 1940s, and its invention was announced in 1948. But its use in computers did not occur until the latter part of the 1950s, and very high volume usage in computers did not occur until the 1960s. This long period of gestation was necessary because translating an invention from the laboratory to the factory floor is an extremely arduous and lengthy process.

The learning process required when a new product or technology is introduced is based on the degree of technical understanding that already exists. If little knowledge exists of the sciences that are the foundation of these processes, management will find it virtually impossible to perform these processes and reproduce them with reasonable uniformity and yield. How do they gain this knowledge? They obtain it through a scientific understanding of the physics, chemistry, and metallurgy of the process, as well as a long and rigorous learning period.

The learning process involves a great deal of fundamental technical knowledge, a lengthy experimentation phase, constant revisions in the product design, and finally an extensive period of production. This early manufacturing phase is needed to help in understanding how the process and the tools operate together and how the process can finally be reproduced repetitively in high-volume manufacture with a high yield. At the beginning of this learning period, the limited degree of understanding of the product and process results in a great deal of instability. The processes are not very reproducible, and the yield is low. We label processes in this unstable condition *soft*. The existence of soft processes in high technology industries is widespread. Because of the intense competitiveness in these industries, new and insufficiently proven processes are constantly introduced into production lines. These new and soft processes are required to increase product performance and decrease cost. It is not unusual for a manufacturer to introduce a small number of soft processes into a mature production line where most of the process steps have reached a high level of learning. The number of these steps may constitute a small fraction of the overall line. Yet the existence of these processes, particularly in the earlier phase of production, can have a devastating impact on cycle time. Under competitive pressure, management is often forced to introduce these new processes or products prematurely, underestimating the extent of technology softness and instability. As a result, it plans an insufficient level of equipment capacity to produce the required product volume.

Not only are processes subject to a lengthy period of softness, but equipment used to carry out these processes encounter the same problem. Practically any piece of machinery, whether it is a simple mechanical tool or a jet airplane, must pass an extensive and lengthy period of testing. This testing must ensure that the parts fit, the materials are sound, the dimensions and tolerances are satisfactory, and the entire assembly of parts works reliably for long periods. Only the most courageous daredevil would have volunteered to be a passenger on the first test flight of the first commercial jet aircraft under development. The jet engine and the jet airplane certainly represent some of the most reliable and rugged machines in the history of mankind. But many years, even decades, of military and civilian testing of the most exhaustive kind preceded the first jet aircraft in service.

Compared to the jet airplane or the space shuttle, installing the first tools on the factory floor is not a life or death matter. Nevertheless, the learning period for machinery on the factory floor can be long and intensive. The queue time of the production line is greatly influenced by the softness of new equipment installed for the first time. This softness exists until a long and difficult learning period is completed. The most complex pieces of equipment, of course, need the longest period of learning. The most difficult problems occur when a new piece of equipment must perform a new and unproven process. The development engineers who have created this process in the laboratory would strongly object to any inference that their process has not been proven.

But there is one lesson that many companies in technology industries have learned after a long and difficult experience: when a machine is performing chemical and metallurgical processes, there is a very strong interaction between the machine and the process. Until this interaction is understood, and until the machine and the process operate as a total compatible system, the results can be disastrous. The manufacturer can learn very little about this interaction in the library or even in the laboratory. It is always possible to make a few parts on a laboratory tool with good results. The proof that it can be made successfully in a laboratory a few times is an extremely important prerequisite to ultimate success in manufacturing. Still, this is only the beginning of the development process, not the end. The marriage of these machines and processes, particularly in high technology industries, must be carried out over a long period of time. This marriage requires extensive equipment debugging under production conditions, changes and optimization of the processes and refinements, even design changes, in the equipment. This period must also involve the accumulation of vast amounts of data so that the manufacturer can monitor the true state of the equipment and process. During this long process of introduction, which can extend for many months, even years, the equipment is clearly soft. The failure to recognize this softness in the planning of a production line will have the same effect as the lack of recognition of the softness of the process— long and costly queues in the line.

Equipment and process learning and softness are facts of life on any new product and technology. They are the price that must be paid for rapidly advancing technology. But the price need not be high. Some simple and relatively inexpensive measures can be taken to compensate for softness and significantly shorten the costly lengthy queues that greatly limit productivity.

The first lesson to be learned is that the introduction into a production line of a new tool and a new process simultaneously can be very risky. The introduction of a new tool *or* a new process with little production experience will require a great deal of work before either can be brought under control. But the introduction of both at the same time compounds the learning problem significantly. If possible, the process should be learned for an extensive period on a tool on which extensive production experience already exists. Once the process is sufficiently understood and under control, the newer tool can be introduced into the line to go through its learning period with a process that has already been stabilized.

Despite this rational and methodical approach to introducing a new tool and process set into production, it may be completely impossible to use it. Competitors will simply not wait until you have carefully redesigned your product and tested it for months or years until you are absolutely sure that everything is perfect in your production line. Under cost, customer, and competitive pressure, every manufacturer is forced to take these risks. The ones who can take risks prudently will be the most successful.

An alternate course of action seems amazingly simple, but many controllers may consider it too expensive. This course involves the addition of small parallel increments of equipment and manpower at critical stages to perform the process during this learning period. By the strategic addition of this equipment and manpower during the phase-in of new processes, the total resource applied to this new process will result in meeting production schedules. If this course of action is so simple, why isn't it followed? For an answer, we return to our bottleneck story. A manufacturing plan is based on a set of assumptions that are often fictitious. Nobody who is engineering a new product is willing to admit that yields will be low, that processes and tools are underdeveloped, or that tools must be purchased that may have to be scrapped five years from now. When a company is besieged by competition and tight profitability problems, it takes a great deal of courage, and possibly independent wealth, for an employee to tell this story to his management. Yet the problem should not be that difficult. There are two lessons management must learn. First, the softness problem of new processes and equipment is a fact of life in an era of rapidly advancing technology and accelerating competition. Second, the price that must be paid for the strategic addition of a limited number of tools and labor during the early learning period of a new technology or process will be incrementally very small compared to the value of the greater output of product and lower costs. It is clearly foolhardy and false economy to believe that saving the costs of these increments of resource saves money. These lower expenditures may help solve this year's bottom line and enhance some executive bonuses, but they may result in next year's catastrophe.

There are two other major causes of long queues. Two important activities in any manufacturing line are *rework* and *inspection*. Many production lines have the capability to rework parts that are defective or do not completely meet specifications. Reworking a part to achieve the necessary specifications can not only restore the part to acceptable quality but also cost significantly less than throwing the part away and making a new one. But estimating the degree of rework needed in a production line is very difficult. The underestimation of this rework factor can seriously impede a production line if there is inadequate rework capacity. This inadequacy will result in a huge bottleneck and constitutes another major cause of long queues.

The second activity that can cause long queues is inspection. Most production lines depend on a great amount of inspection to ensure that the product is meeting specifications at several steps of the manufacturing process. There is often a tendency for management to underestimate the degree of inspection required. This underestimation, like that of rework, is also responsible for extensive bottlenecks and lengthened cycle time. (Both rework and inspection are so important to the manufacturing process that chapter 10 is devoted to them.)

We have covered four serious causes of large queues and high cycle time: soft tools, soft processes, rework, and inspection. The manufacturing manager who tries to wish these phenomena away and pretend that shortcuts can inexpensively avoid them is likely to do so at great risk with serious consequences.

Another common disease causes long queues; it is much simpler in concept than the four already discussed: this malady is called *one-of-a-kind tools*. In many production lines, certain tools have throughput capacities that are far in excess of the planned throughput through its sector. If the plan, for example, is to process 1,000 parts each hour and the tool is capable of processing 2,000 per hour, most controllers will observe that with only one piece of equipment, there will still be excess capacity. A less costly piece of equipment could be purchased that would have a capacity of only 1,000 per hour or, to play it safe, 1,300 per hour. This reasoning is correct, *providing the tool can work 100 percent of the time*. But when can any manufacturer of even the simplest of products with the most elementary of tools recall when a machine could run with 100 percent availability and utilization? In reality, even after a complex machine has passed through its learning phase and has passed from the category of soft to hard, utilization factors of 60 to 70 percent at best can be expected. Thus, during the 30 to 40 percent of the time when the machine is being repaired or serviced, inventory will accumulate in large quantities, waiting for the machine to be operating on the line again. Each time this lone tool is down for repairs, a major bottleneck is created, a long queue of parts is formed, and the cycle time is greatly increased. The solution to this problem is obvious: buy a second tool. Of course, nobody likes to see a tool underutilized; it seems like a waste of money. But the greater the number of tools, the greater the probability that when the parts come down the line to a work station, a tool will be ready to process them. The incremental cost of that extra tool will be far more than offset by the shorter queues that will result, the shorter cycle time, and the increased output.

Queue Time: Influence of Scheduling, Tracking, and Prioritizing Jobs

Most manufacturing managers believe that enough work should be provided for all work areas to avoid any idle manufacturing capacity. It is necessary, they hold, to ensure that all equipment and manpower capacity that makes up the value add time is fully utilized. In seeking to ensure full utilization, there is a great temptation to overschedule these work stations. The problem with this overscheduling is that it results in excessive work-in-process waiting at each sector of the line. The more work piled onto the line, the greater the number of partially completed products waiting in queues. Large inventories of partially completed products waiting in queues at successive work centers have a predictable impact on productivity: jobs get completed later and later. Since the capacity at the work centers to process the increasing number of parts is limited, all that has been done is the increase of the cycle time and work-in-process inventory. The managers have convinced themselves that the tools and people are working at capacity, but the product isn't getting out any faster or in any larger quantities.

To compensate for the lateness of the products coming out of the line, the next temptation, equally difficult to resist, is to start more jobs earlier. But what does this action accomplish? It serves only to add work to the existing queues, which in turn makes jobs already late—even later. If this mode of operation is carried further, a vicious cycle begins of earlier and earlier job starts with later and later job completions.

It is easy to recognize a production operation in which the production control and manufacturing managers overschedule the line to keep the work centers busy. The most common feature is a large work-in-process bubble at the beginning and a relatively light load of parts toward the end where the work is completed. This condition results from a number of bottlenecks at various sectors. While management is aggressively feeding parts into the lines, with the hope that production will speed up, bottlenecks are simply preventing the parts from moving any faster.

The problem of queues and bottlenecks is significantly complicated by more process steps. In many products, such as those we have labeled high technology, as many as several hundred individual steps must be carried out in the construction of the final product. As these technologies advance in performance and complexity, the number of process steps will continue to increase. In this type of manufacture, constant changes in requirements and priorities are a way of life. For example, consider the case of a component known as product A that will be used in an electronic system called product Z to be built by another manufacturer. Product A must go through a long learning process during the early stages of manufacture. During this period, constant changes will be made in design and process. These changes must be continuously tested to determine if they work. At the same time, product Z must also undergo a learning period that will require constant design modifications. These changes will place different demands on the design of product A. While the manufacturer of A is learning new processes, it must also respond to the changes required by the manufacturer of Z. In a production line making product A with hundreds of different process steps, the volatility created by all of these changes can create total chaos if the line isn't managed correctly. In this environment, logistics becomes very important. Managers must be able to track and prioritize jobs in the line. They must know at all times where the parts are coming from, their location, and where they want them to go.

Earlier in this chapter, we recommended that a multiprocess line should be divided into sectors so that its performance can be analyzed in such a way that chronic bottlenecks can be located. Performing such an analysis becomes increasingly important with lines of increasing complexity and becomes a necessity when the line exceeds ten or twelve operations. This division into sectors becomes essential, not only for the detection of imbalances but also for tracking the line performance. In a line of the type of complexity encountered in high technology, any attempt to track the state of the product without a systematic tracking system would be practically impossible.

In most high technology industries where advanced tracking systems have been implemented, the product is monitored when it enters and when it leaves each sector. This *sector level tracking system* permits us to identify and find solutions to chronic bottlenecks. This approach provides a powerful method of balancing the line to improve productivity through increasing capacity utilization. Sector-level tracking alone, however, may not lead to easy identification and solution of bottlenecks, when sectors consist of a number of manufacturing operations. In these complex operations, it becomes difficult to identify either a substandard level of performance by an operator or a tool that is encountering difficulties.

An example of this problem can be found in a process known as lithography in the manufacturing of semiconductor chips. The lithography sector consists of several individual operations, including applying a photoresist material, baking, optical exposure, developing, and visual inspection. The problem can be further aggravated if the same equipment is used at different points of the manufacturing line. Furthermore, the difficulties can be complicated if the product is recycled at these sectors. For example, in our lithography example, it may be necessary to rework some of the product if it is found to be defective at this point of the process. This rework is accomplished by stripping the photoresist material and repeating the same sequence of operations.

Multiple operations at a sector, use of the same equipment at different points of the process, and recycling of the product resulting from the need to perform rework can create a great deal of confusion. But this confusion can be greatly minimized by adopting a further refinement in the tracking system. This refinement consists of tracking at the operation level, as well as monitoring the operator performance at a particular manufacturing operation. A wide variety of optical, magnetic, and electronic systems makes this type of tracking technically and economically feasible. These systems are available on the market today and can be easily implemented. With this type of system, critical chronic bottleneck operations can be quickly identified with a minimum of confusion. Manpower skill problems and shortages can be identified and solved.

The third important aspect of running the line is prioritizing jobs. Many industries today have a continuous need to make process and design changes throughout the life of the product. Some of these changes are required for the learning process of a high technology component. Others may be needed to accommodate changes in the equipment or system where the component is destined to be used, and some may be required to accommodate a changing customer requirement. These changes must be made much more rapidly than the normal cycle time of the standard product. Expediting these jobs through a fully loaded production line by giving them priority is a very difficult task. Not only is it difficult to process these jobs quickly, but expediting them can have a disruptive effect on the remainder of the product making its way through the line.

To understand these difficulties we revert to our often-used traffic analogies. Police cars, ambulances, and fire engines always have priority in traffic over all other vehicles in case of an emergency. Picture a three-lane highway in the middle of the night when there is very little traffic. An ambulance would have no difficulty rushing past the few vehicles on the road and going to its destination practically unimpeded. Now consider the same three-lane highway with bumper-to-bumper traffic on all three lanes. The ambulance, sirens blasting and lights flashing, signals that it is responding to an emergency and must therefore demand its right of priority. Cars in the vicinity of the ambulance slow down and move to the right or left to make whatever room is available so that the emergency vehicle can squeeze by. As the ambulance progresses, similar actions are taken by the drivers then in its vicinity; traffic almost comes to a halt in order to facilitate the ambulance. Now imagine the chaos that would result if every few minutes a priority vehicle were to disrupt the flow of traffic that already suffered from bottlenecks due to toll booths, bridges, accidents, or lanes closed for repair work.

The effect of prioritizing jobs in a fully loaded manufacturing line is very similar to moving priority vehicles in traffic afflicted by bottlenecks. But why are job priorities used in manufacturing if their effect can be so negative? Their use is not only very tempting but also at times necessary. The pressure to push through products at a faster rate to serve a particular customer need or to quickly get answers to engineering problems can be very great.

Two further aspects to job prioritization make the effect of this practice even more serious. Priorities are normally used when jobs are already late. These jobs are late usually because of poor scheduling of the work or insufficient capacity. The effect of prioritizing late jobs in such a constrained line is similar to moving a priority vehicle in traffic already encountering bottlenecks. The effect on the performance of nonpriority jobs can be severe. The second problem relates to management's perception of how effective prioritization can be. Even under the worst of circumstances, the prioritized job will be completed faster than the others. Isn't it reasonable to expect that if we prioritize more jobs, we will process more jobs faster through the line? In our traffic analogy, why allow only ambulances, fire engines, and police cars priority? Shouldn't we speed up the whole process by awarding the same privilege to all doctors, lawyers, diplomats, and perhaps even politicians? An infrequent use of priority jobs can often be effective with a minimum of disruption to the remainder of the jobs in a production line. However, the abuse of priorities by escalating the number of jobs that are given this privilege can be extremely disruptive. In our experience, the average cycle time and throughput performance of a manufacturing line degrades exponentially as the percentage of priority jobs loads the line to a level approaching its effective capacity.

Does all this mean that jobs should never be prioritized? Although a penalty is paid in the sacrifice of overall production when preference is given to some jobs, the price may often be worth paying. During the early phases of introduction of a new product into manufacturing, many process modifications and engineering changes will be required to bring the product to its specified level of performance. If the manufacturing cycles are long, it may be necessary to make engineering changes in the shortest possible time so that these changes can be quickly verified. Product introduction may actually require several iterations of changes before the ultimate customer specifications are met. The faster these changes are introduced, the sooner the manufacturer can get to the marketplace and compete. There are methods that can be applied to achieve relatively fast cycle times for prioritized parts with minimum reduction in cycle time for the bulk of production. The most effective, although the most expensive, is to build a completely separate line exclusively devoted to the processing of high-priority parts. Such a separate line would be analogous to the construction of a separate lane on a highway, totally dedicated to the use of emergency vehicles. A second, less costly, method would be to operate the line considerably below its capacity, either by reducing the output of product or by increasing the number of tools and manpower at critical sectors. This method is less costly than the dedicated line but would be less effective in achieving a low cycle time.

Of course, like all investments, the choice of approaches is a trade-off between cost and need. In some industries, particularly high technology, long learning periods and the need for extensive engineering and process changes demand the lowest possible cycle times. The higher-cost alternative could result in overall savings resulting from higher revenues and more successful competitiveness.

10
Managing Learning

Rework and Inspection: What Can Go Wrong?

In the simplest of manufacturing processes something will always go wrong. The probability that all parts that begin the process will emerge from the end of the line without a defect is very low. As the processes become more numerous and complex, this probability decreases even further; it would be foolhardy to assume otherwise. We have discussed yield several times in this book. Yield is a good measure of the parts that fall out of the line as rejects. Yield has little meaning in a mechanical assembly process because if a part is defective it can be rejected from the assembly and a good part substituted. In high technology manufacture, though, such as integrated circuits, which may involve several hundred process steps, a defect at one step can reject the entire part. Because of the high chemical and metallurgical content of these processes, there are few places where we can remove a completed step and repeat it again. (There are some notable exceptions, however—processes that can in fact be repeated many times, or *reworked*.)

As has been explained, yield learning is a slow, tedious, and methodical process that may take as long as several years. To reach the highest yield consistent with our knowledge and control of the technology, management suffers through long periods of trial and error, changes in tools and processes, adjustment of specifications, and extensive training of personnel. This yield learning is traditionally factored into manufacturing plans because it is generally recognized throughout industry that this is a fact of technology life and cannot be avoided.

The Rework Learning Curve

We have used the photolithography process in manufacturing semiconductors as an example of how rework can be an economic and technically viable alternative to throwing away the product and starting all over again. Many high technology products, as well as those of other types of industries, have examples of such rework. The simple and economic measures discussed here can greatly increase productivity of all of them.

Although yield learning is accepted and accommodated in planning, rework is not normally understood to be learned. In high technology many processes permanently alter the state of the product; the operation cannot be reversed, repeated, or repaired. In fact, most processes in high technology manufacture fall into that category. Some processes, however, can be repeated by removing material and carrying out the process again.

The manufacture of semiconductor circuits, for example, contains several points in its process where rework can be carried out without adverse impact on product yield or quality. In the manufacture of integrated silicon circuits, many devices such as transistors are interconnected on the silicon wafer using chemical and photolithographical operations to imprint the circuit pattern. A typical series consists of applying a photoresist polymer material, baking, performing an optical exposure, developing, and then visually inspecting the product. The primary purpose of this inspection is to determine the quality of the circuit pattern. During the visual inspection, the pattern is magnified several hundred times, if necessary, to detect any irregularities in the pattern structure. If the inspector determines that the pattern is unsatisfactory, the wafer is rejected and returned for rework. In the rework operation, the photoresist is first stripped from the wafer. The wafer is cleaned, and the same series of operations from application of the resist material to visual inspection is repeated again. If the inspection reveals no additional problems, the wafer resumes the process. If another defect is discovered, the wafer is returned again for rework. In fact, this process can be repeated almost indefinitely without penalty to the yield or reliability of the product. Why don't we just throw away the wafer and avoid the expense of the rework operation? By the time the wafer reaches this stage of the line, much expense has been incurred. The incremental cost of reworking it several times is small compared to the total cost of processing up to that point. Of course, there is a limit to the number of times the product can be economically reworked, but this limit is seldom reached.

The ability to reduce the number of times a product must be reworked in this manner depends on an understanding of the materials, processes, and tools used to perform these operations. These processes must be learned. In the same manner that management must go through a learning period to increase yield, it must plan on a learning curve on rework. One of the major driving forces in high technology products is the effort to manufacture these products at increasingly high densities—that is, more and more circuits in a given unit of area of silicon. These higher densities are required to achieve lower cost and higher circuit speed. More complex processes are required to achieve these higher integration levels. Such complex processes often require the use of new materials and advanced equipment. Until these new processes are learned, high levels of rework will be necessary. As the manufacturer traverses the learning curve, competitive forces will result in further advances in technology requiring further complexity and learning. These increases in complexity force constant learning in both yields and rework.

During the early stage of manufacturing of a new process, manufacturing management usually underestimates the rework it expects to experience. First, development engineers use relaxed criteria for visual inspection because their motivation is to establish that the product works and achieves the desired level of performance. At this early stage of the technology life, there is little direct concern for ultimate cost or even reliability. Manufacturing, on the other hand, will ultimately need to use much stricter criteria. The product must conform to tight specifications and operate at very high levels of reliability. A temptation exists, however, to use the development laboratory experience in planning manufacturing capacity.

A second reason that rework is underestimated is management's view of rework. Rework is considered a very negative word. It means that something is wrong. In an era where the slogan "doing things right the first time" is accepted as a desirable, even mandatory goal, rework is not acceptable to management. It does not tolerate high rework, orders its elimination, and insists that capital, manpower, and engineering resources be planned on the assumption that little or no rework will be needed. Manufacturing management believes that if low levels of rework can be achieved in development, for whatever reason, manufacturing should be able to do the same. Of course, management should insist that rework should be eliminated in the same way that it should insist on 100 percent yield or zero defects. But it should also realize that these goals may take years to achieve. In a fast-moving competitive world, they may never be achieved, as each advance takes the place of the previous one and sets a new learning goal to be obtained.

While management pursues these difficult and elusive goals, it should realize that rework constitutes a major reason for manufacturing bottlenecks in high technology. We can best illustrate the rework bottleneck problem by considering a hypothetical, but by no means unrealistic, example. The manufacturer begins production of a product that requires 70 percent rework. This means that for every 100 parts processed through certain sectors of the line, 70 do not pass the inspection satisfactorily and must be reworked through the same set of process steps. It is immediately obvious that if additional capacity in the rework operation is not planned for, parts will collect in a queue and a bottleneck will form. It would appear obvious that this could be solved simply by adding 70 percent capacity in tools and personnel to eliminate the bottleneck. Let us test this solution by considering what actually happens to the parts that have been reworked.

The 70 parts that have been reworked have passed through the same set of processes through which the first 100 parts passed. Because the same effectiveness of the process existed for the 70 reworked parts, 70 percent of them, or 49 parts, will again return for rework. When these 49 parts are reworked, inspection will reject 70 percent of them or approximately 34 parts. For each successive rework cycle, 70 percent of the remaining parts will be rejected until there are no longer any parts to be reworked. By the time these cycles have been completed, not 70 parts but a total of 230 will have been reworked. In other words, the number is determined by an arithmetic series.[1] To prevent a bottleneck from occurring, we must provide for an additional capacity of 2.3 times the original capacity of 100 parts.

No manufacturer can accept for the life of a product a 70 percent level for rework. But for complex technological products, that level of rework at the beginning of the production experience is not at all unusual. The learning of the process through extensive production experience will ultimately lower the level of rework. It is thus not unusual in high technology products, such as integrated circuits, for production to begin with a 50 to 70 percent rework or even more and eventually reach levels of 10 percent or less. During this learning period, the manufacturing executive has two options. One is to mandate that production operations achieve a low level of rework from the beginning and then ignore the gigantic bottlenecks that pile up while productivity takes a nose-dive and costs escalate. The other option is to add sufficient capacity at the beginning of the production cycle to accommodate the high level of rework. This might appear to the controller to be a costly, even irresponsible, proposal. But the incremental costs of adding the small amount of equipment and personnel to handle the extra rework capacity are very small compared to the price in high work-in-process inventory and low output of product. Furthermore, most production lines begin at relatively low levels of volume for a new product. As the product volumes increase and the rework levels decrease, the increment of equipment required for the total production cycle can be very small.

The Inspection Learning Curve

Inspection is a major part of manufacturing. Managers cannot assume that foolproof manufacturing processes exist, particularly in the early life of a product. They want to know the physical state of the product, not only after it is completed but also while they make it. If problems creep into the production line, and if these problems affect quality, cost, or performance, they don't want to wait a long time for the bad news. They need to know immediately so that they can reject defective parts and take quick action to solve the problem that caused them. Inspecting is an important part of the production process. But inspection can be overdone. The reduction of inspections must be a continuous goal of manufacturing management. It is costly and impedes productivity.

During the development of a new product or process, inspections are instituted to assist the engineer and production employees in understanding the effect of a new operation. They need to understand the behavior of a new process, by itself and in combination with other processes. As the learning phase proceeds, visual inspections and measurements are needed to determine the effectiveness of each new step. As processes become more numerous and complex, the number of inspections increase. In fact, engineers often add an inspection step and, where possible, a measurement whenever they add a new process. Engineers need a great deal of information to determine the status of the process change. They must have a good indicator of the value of the change, as well as what additional modifications must be made. There is, however, a tendency for engineers to institute an inspection or measurement even when there appears to be little value in them.

For reasons of good economics, the manufacturer would like to reject a bad product as early in the production process as possible before committing more cost to it, particularly if that product will ultimately be thrown away. This economic reason and the need for process change information often justify the introduction of inspections and measurements. In many products that are manufactured by a long series of operations, one operation could introduce a defect that could cripple that piece and doom it to eventual rejection. Early in the life of a product, during the early learning phase, large defects are often easy to inspect visually. The engineer installs an inspection step to inspect for these gross defects. But after the product begins to be brought under control, these obvious defects become less of a problem, and the remaining defects are too small to detect visually. In fact, in many high technology products, some defects are practically invisible, even to the most sensitive inspection equipment. Yet these submicroscopic flaws can render the product inoperable or, at best, of poor quality. Although there is no practical way to detect the presence of the defect at the point when it is introduced, an electrical measurement made much later in the production process will reveal that the defect has, in fact, destroyed the product. Nevertheless, despite the questionable value of the inspection step, engineers are reluctant to eliminate it.

With the precise inspection and measurement equipment now available, the engineer and foreman tend to inspect and measure everything, to "play it safe." There is a danger that inspections and measurements will grow like a monster and become an excessive preoccupation in a production line. In the manufacture of many products, it is not uncommon to find one-half or more of the labor force engaged in inspection and measurements. Much of this high level of activity is associated with the rigors of bringing into reality a new and complex technology. There is a natural tendency, however, to maintain these inspections and measurements long after the product has matured—to a point where they are neither economic or technically of value. In an effort to control the process through the use of inspections, the engineer often attributes improvements in yield to the inspection process itself.

Even in the most disciplined manufacturing plants, these factors keep the inspection percentages well above the planned levels. The complexity of the processes, the volatility of the development and early production phases, and the constant changes in design all combine to make it difficult to properly estimate the level of inspection that will be needed. The combination of large numbers of inspections and measurements can have a severe impact on the cycle time. An even greater problem occurs when the resources planned for inspection and measurement are too low to cope with the actual levels.

Management looks with equal disfavor on high levels of inspection and measurement and on rework. This attitude results in planning for a low inspection and measurement level (5 to 10 percent) even though the actual number, particularly early in the program, will be 25 to 50 percent. The effect of this unrealistic planning is the creation of severe bottlenecks simply because the resource is not available to perform the inspection operations. With the shortage of equipment and personnel for inspection and measurement, product piles up in inventory, severely limiting manufacturing throughput.

We don't believe in excessive inspection. The disapproving attitude of management toward this excess is justifiable. Management must require a continuous and detailed examination of the technical need and economic justification for all inspection and measurement steps. Every effort should continuously be made to reduce the level of inspection in the production line. But management should also recognize that, like rework and yield, there is a learning process for inspections. In products of increasing technological complexity, this learning process cannot be avoided. In the meantime, management must maintain the levels of resource that are consistent with actual experience. Like rework and yield, the price they must pay for that extra resource is small compared to increased productivity, increased output, and reduced cycle time.

11
Productivity Techniques for an Unconstrained Environment

T he highest productivity dividends are attained in a constrained environment where a small increment in resources, applied in the right places, can result in major increases in production. But all businesses aren't fortunate enough to exist in this privileged state of ever-increasing demand for their products. Even the most successful growth companies face cyclical or seasonal swings in demand. Furthermore, every industry and company experiences the vicissitudes caused by economic recessions, foreign competition, resource disruptions, and even the weather. For all of these reasons, and many others, industries at one time or another operate in an unconstrained environment where no immediate additional demand exists for their products.

Every business manager or factory executive who runs an unconstrained operation wants to run lean and mean. He wants to cut overhead, labor, and capital costs to the bone. Excesses in all of these categories are heavy baggage to carry, but how does the manager know which baggage to unload?

Some of the same productivity techniques that we have described for constrained operations can be applied to the unconstrained ones. Before discussing the techniques that can best be used in these operations, it is worth repeating the goals for manufacturing discussed in an earlier chapter. The five primary purposes of any production line are:

↑ Throughput

↓ Inventory

↓ Operating expense

↓ Cycle time

↑ Yield (especially applicable to high technology)

In an unconstrained operation, where no additional demand exists for the product, increased throughput is obviously not an objective. But these are precisely the circumstances in which inventory costs and operating expense can be reduced without too much risk. The failure of the U.S. industrial system to reduce inventories and operating expenses, particularly when the risk is minimal, has been a major cause for poor U.S. productivity performance.

Inventory can be measured in two ways. First, the actual work-in-process inventory should be compared to the planned inventory. The planned inventory is simply the product of the planned throughput and the cycle time:

$$\text{planned inventory} = \text{planned throughput} \times \text{cycle time}$$

In an unconstrained production line, the planned throughput is lower than the capacity of the line, and consequently the planned inventory will be lower. Another measure of inventory is *inventory turnover:*

$$\text{inventory turnover} = \frac{\text{cost of goods sold}}{\text{cost of average inventory}}$$

The capacity of a factory represents the maximum practical amount of output that can be produced with the current equipment. If the plant is not constrained, it is characterized by surplus capacity and a low-capacity utilization rate.

If reduction of inventories is a major step that must be taken to raise productivity in an unconstrained operation, how is this intermediate goal accomplished? We have consistently emphasized the need to reduce bottlenecks in a constrained factory. In the case of an unconstrained factory, we propose initially to do just the opposite—that is, to create bottlenecks using the following technique. First, the work-in-process inventory levels should be gradually and continuously reduced by decreasing the inline buffers—that is, the inventory of parts waiting at each sector. These reductions can be made by reducing the release of parts into the line so that entry of raw materials rebalances the line by moving resources into sectors that have excess inventory. Those sections of the line having the highest actual inventory ratios are the first targets for reduction. While this work-in-process inventory is being reduced, the cycle time and throughput levels for each sector should be constantly monitored against the planned targets.

This process of reducing the inventory levels should be continued until it actually creates a bottleneck. If the bottleneck is a temporary rather than a chronic condition, temporary resources should be allocated to remove it: overtime, weekends, extra shifts, or the movement of resources from operations with surplus manpower can be used.

Of course, actions taken to eliminate the bottlenecks cost money. But the extra expense incurred by moving temporary resources may be small compared to the cost of carrying an excessive inventory, particularly in industries where the cost of raw materials is high.

Once this temporary bottleneck is removed inventory is again lowered in search of the next bottleneck. Once again the focus is on those sectors with the greatest excess inventory. This process continues until one or more sectors of the line either becomes a chronic bottleneck or simply can no longer meet the planned throughput level due to the lack of inventory. If a chronic bottleneck has been created, resources should be permanently allocated to that sector to remove this chronic condition, and inventory should again be reduced. If the inventory levels have already reached levels that are too low to meet the planned throughput, further reduction should be stopped.

Before resuming this cycle of inventory reduction and bottleneck creation, the overall state of the line should be closely examined so that the area of greatest excess work-in-process inventory can be identified and allocated resources.

How long should this cycle be continued? It should be repeated as long as it is economically feasible. Management must consider several factors—the desired inventory turnover ratio, the expense of solving the bottlenecks versus the cost of carrying the inventory, and the ability to manage the cycle times—before the cycle is halted.

In practice, additional expense to solve the bottlenecks created in this way is seldom required in an unconstrained environment. In virtually every case, only a rebalancing of resources is required, and this rebalancing is achieved by reallocating labor, maintenance, and engineering personnel from areas that have excess capacity.

By repeating this process, managers can achieve the objective of lowering inventory and cycle times. But how can they lower expenses? An obvious opportunity is the reduction of overhead. The almost endless number of targets of opportunity for trimming includes engineering, sales, administration, benefits, advertising, salaries. Trimming is essential if a production operation is going to be lean and mean. But lean does not necessarily make us mean; in fact, cutting in the wrong places could make the operation lean and weak. Misdirected false economies can have disastrous long-term consequences. Businesses tend to run fat during periods of prosperity. When the economy takes a downturn or severe competition threatens market share, management may bring out the meat axe and sharply reduce its resources, with serious consequences. Both extremes are unnecessary and dangerous. Any resource reduction should be carried out with discipline and systematically. The methods of reducing inventories and reallocation of resources that have been discussed in this chapter are examples of how this balancing and resource reduction should be carried out.

A word of caution must be given regarding the management of critical personnel of any industry, whether constrained or unconstrained. These people may include engineers, technicians, management, maintenance, personnel, administrators, scientists, and direct labor workers, many of whom have priceless skills and experience. It may take only one day to get rid of them, but many years to replace them. Losing these critical resources can result in a devastating long-term price in return for a short-term relief on this year's bottom line. How many companies have resorted to such practices as layoffs, stopping professional hiring, and even mass firings of critical personnel in the face of economic uncertainty? In many cases, on later reflection, the same management regretted these precipitous and misguided actions.

It is not easy for management to forgo short-term economies in return for longer-term prosperity. But maintaining continuity of critical skills in any company is a major prerequisite to increasing productivity. U.S. management, shareholders, financial markets, and the general public need to take a longer-term view of company performance.

12
Preventing Productivity Problems: Manufacturing Line Architecture

T he discussion so far has focused on methods of improving productivity in existing production lines. We have demonstrated
how to increase throughput and decrease inventory levels and
cycle time through line balancing. We have also shown how learning
curves for rework and inspection can be factored into manufacturing
planning in such a way that bottlenecks can be prevented during the
learning period of a product. But if the architecture of a production line
can be defined using these methods before the line is built, the ability to
increase productivity can be greatly improved.

Architecture is the art and science of designing and erecting build-
ings. In fact, however, it can be more broadly defined as the art and
science of designing and erecting anything. It is "any design or orderly
arrangement perceived by man."[1] Before a building or a production line
is constructed, an architect must design it in an orderly way.

Naturally, the word *architecture* is usually applied to the design of
a building. But this chapter discusses the architecture of a production
line, not only the structure that houses it but the design and arrangement
of the line itself. There are, however, some analogies between the architecture of a production line and that of a building. Everyone has a vision
of a dream house, with a concept of the number, size, shape, and arrangement of the rooms. Fitting this concept into an existing building
would most likely have little success. The floor plan would be constrained by the fixed sizes and shapes of the rooms. Even if all of the
inside walls were torn down, any attempt to construct the rooms according to this design would probably face some serious limitations. The
rooms would be smaller, or they would be shaped and arranged differ-
ently, than the ideal concept. The entry would be directly into the living
room instead of the central foyer that had to be eliminated from the
plans. Closet space might be reduced, and the upstairs bathroom might
end up at the wrong end of the hall. But if an architect is hired to design
a new house, the concept can be turned into reality.

The problems of constructing a factory are different from those of building a house. Nevertheless, the need for an architecture is equally as important. If the factory is not designed in an orderly arrangement, the result can be a hodge-podge of tools with low productivity.

Some methods of productivity in existing production lines have already been discussed. Like designing a floor plan in an existing house, however, there are constraints in improving productivity in a factory with such lines. Using the methods described, adding tools and people for the purpose of balancing the production line may be limited by lack of space. If tools are placed in a remote area where space exists, flow of work may be disturbed. Despite the constraints of an existing building, using the methods of bottleneck elimination discussed in this book in current production lines have proven effective in improving productivity. But the building and the production line designed in advance of their construction would reduce these constraints, provide a much greater degree of flexibility in the line, and further help improve the line's productivity. Of course, few, if any, companies can afford to build a new building every time they change products or processes. They can, however, structure their plant so that it is flexible enough to accommodate many future changes.

What Will the Factory Build?

Before designing a house, the architect must know how many people are expected to live in it. Before designing a factory, the products to be manufactured in it and the market demand for the product must be defined. Once the products have been determined, the two most important considerations are the design of the product and the process required to build it. The design of the product and the methods by which it will be produced have a major effect on the cost and competitiveness. The most productive factory concept cannot compensate for an inefficient and noncompetitively designed product. In many products there is a trend toward increasing complexity. This complexity is fostered by a need to achieve higher performance and reliability. In order to meet competitive costs, the manufacturer must often make tradeoffs among the objectives of improved performance, reliability, and cost. Sometimes one of these objectives can be achieved without sacrificing the other two; frequently a compromise must be obtained among these three objectives.

After product and process design are defined, there is a great temptation to continually increase the complexity and length of the manufacturing process. The engineer may add process steps to improve yield. The manufacturing and quality control management may increase the number of inspections and measurement points. There may be good reasons that justify these additions, but the effect on productivity can be very serious.

In discussing manufacturing line architecture, it is assumed that management has met all of the above prerequisites, including the choice of products, process, and tools. Once these decisions are made, the design of the production line can begin.

Process Flexibility

A factory can't be efficiently designed without knowing what products will be built in it. Nor can the architecture for the plant be easily developed if the planned products are expected to change substantially. This problem is particularly serious in high-technology industries. High technology is advancing at a breathtaking pace: it is one of the major growth areas for the remainder of this century and well into the next. Furthermore, the number of applications and the products using these technologies are spiraling out of sight. The foundation of this phenomenal growth has been the processes used to manufacture high technology products. Major investments in research and development are essential if a company is to successfully compete in this industry. But this investment alone is far from sufficient. The success or failure of a company depends on its ability to master the manufacture of these products. This mastery will determine who will achieve superiority and who will fail in this high-stakes technical environment.

One consequence of this technological race is the great volatility of the manufacturing process. The intense competition for improved cost and performance of these products forces the manufacturer to engage in a continuous cycle of change. The only way to cope with this competition is to improve the products while manufacturing them, constantly upgrade them, and even replace them with new and superior ones. Successful companies recognize the reality of this constant cycle of change and find ways to plan for it. A conservative manufacturing management usually takes a hard-nosed attitude to change: until research and development can prove the necessity and feasibility of a change, manufacturing will not plan for it. It won't waste time and resources on a development engineer's dream. It will build the factory to accommodate proven processes. Why should unnecessary risks be taken when management has a product that it knows how to make and sell? This cautious attitude is a formula for this year's success and future catastrophe. It is comparable to having a gourmet dinner while the ship is sinking. The progressive companies that recognize this rapid era of change and how to plan for it will quickly eliminate the conservative manufacturer from business.

What can the manufacturer do to cope with such volatility and change? First, it must accept them as facts of life in a highly competitive world. Next, it must recognize that today's engineering dream can become tomorrow's production nightmare if it is not adequately planned for. Finally, the architecture of the future factory must include strategically planned space and facilities for those tools, materials, and chemicals that could become a part of future manufacturing processes. In a production line with hundreds of process steps, changes in only a few critical ones can often pay immense dividends in improvement in product performance. Accommodating these changes may require a relatively small investment of space and capital. Paying for these small increments of resources can pay off handsomely. Saving the expenditure of these relatively small investments can result in disaster. The architecture of a new factory must sensibly provide the resources needed to accommodate any known process currently under development, particularly those having a reasonable chance of success. If management is not willing to provide this flexibility, the savings of a small amount of capital and space will result in the loss of a major competitive opportunity.

How to Avoid a TRIP to Low Production

This chapter has shown how serious manufacturing bottlenecks are created by inadequate planning for new and soft *t*ools, greater than anticipated *r*ework and *i*nspection, and new and soft *p*rocesses. These four important factors, which conveniently create the acronym TRIP, have indeed tripped the manufacturing performance of many production lines. They are particularly important in high technology where the problems created by them are present to a high degree. An earlier discussion explained how we can eliminate bottlenecks created by TRIP on production lines already in existence. But if these factors can be anticipated before the factory is designed, management can greatly improve its ability to cope with them and improve productivity.

Many manufacturing executives and controllers treat extra contingency space and equipment as a serious offense. They regard these as luxuries like a third family automobile, an extra television set, or a bedroom that is used only once a year when grandmother comes to town. But building a factory isn't the same as building a house. Most families survive very well with only two cars or even one. If that extra bedroom doesn't exist, grandmother can sleep on the living room couch or even spend a few nights in a hotel. Preparing for the contingencies that are characteristic of competitive high technologies or even products of lesser complexity is a far more difficult proposition. The architecture of a factory must accommodate these contingency factors as much as possible. Their price is small compared to flexibility and increased productivity.

The four elements of TRIP make up the major uncertainties in planning a factory. The greater the complexity of the product, the greater its uncertainty. Increasing competitiveness forces more rapid and risky innovation, which further increases the volatility of the manufacturing process and increases the exposure due to the TRIP phenomena. How does management cope with these problems? It can be done by carefully examining each of these four areas, and understanding how they will be influenced by the new products and technologies being planned for production. Then careful plans must be made for the extra increments of resources that will be needed to give adequate contingencies in space, manpower, and tools. The architecture of future factories must incorporate these extra resources. There will never be a perfect plan or a precise way to measure the magnitude of these extra resources. But at least it can be recognized that they are needed, and, with a fair degree of approximation, their size can be estimated. Our experience in applying these practices has demonstrated that relatively small increments of capital and manpower (10 percent or less) can result in major (over 100 percent) increases in line throughput with significant reductions in cycle time and inventory.

Part III
Implementing Productivity

13
Case Studies

The seven case studies presented in this chapter demonstrate how major production benefits can be obtained by applying the techniques described in this book. Included here is a wide spectrum of examples of U.S. industries. The case studies show that techniques of identifying and eliminating bottlenecks in a production line can be applied with great success, even in the most complex industries. In fact, these methods can be effective in the manufacture of practically any product. Dramatic increases in product output, accompanied by significant reductions in cycle time and work-in-process inventory, can be achieved with a very small increase in capital and manpower resources.

Table 13–1 tabulates seven categories of industries ranging from relatively stable job shop operations to complex, revolutionary high technology industries. The table also describes several characteristics of each category, such as technology level, degree of product and process change, and cost structure. This chapter includes a case study of each of these seven categories.

We have chosen some key characteristics to describe the nature of the industries classified by the different categories. The classifications— very high, high, medium, low, revolutionary, evolutionary, and stable— are largely arbitrary and are intended as guidelines for establishing a framework within which a company might be operating. The categories and the characteristics listed for each were specifically designed to reflect actual cases and help explain why a particular productivity technique was successful. The definitions of the classifications of the various characteristics used in table 13–1 are briefly described in table 13–2.

Case 1: High Technology and Automation

The first case study is based on an automated production line built by the Autotech Corporation. This line manufactures a high technology component. As described in many parts of this book, these types of production lines are characterized by low manufacturing yields and high

Table 13–1
Characteristics of Seven Industry Categories

	1	2	3
Technology level	High	High	High
Environment			
Product			
Degree of change	Evolutionary	Revolutionary	Evolutionary
Mix variability	High	Medium	Medium
Process			
Degree of change	Evolutionary	Revolutionary	Evolutionary
Stability	Low	Very low	Medium
Control environment			
Mechanization	High	High	High
Automation	High	Medium	Low
Computer control	Very high	Medium	Medium
Logistics control	Very high	High	Medium
Cost structure			
Capital	Very high	Very high	Very high
Labor	Low	Low	Low
Overhead	Very high	Very high	Very high
Material	Low	Low	Low
Product structure			
Component	Yes	Yes	Yes
Sub-assembly		Yes	
Assembly		Yes	
Other characteristics	Low yield	Low yield	Medium yield
	High rework	High rework	Low rework
	High inspection	High inspection	

levels of rework and inspection, particularly during the early years of production.

Autotech automated this line for the purpose of achieving the shortest possible cycle time for these high technology products. The product consists of several hundred different part numbers that must be produced on the same line. More than 100 individual process steps are required to manufacture these products. Their manufacture is further complicated by technology that is continually evolving, resulting in constant design modifications and process improvements.

The Autotech line has accurate logistics control. The product movement is automatically tracked using sensors connected to sensor-based computers. This capability provides almost perfect information on throughput, cycle time, and work-in-process inventory. Most of the tools are highly mechanized, and product is transported from tool to tool by automatic transports.

4	5	6	7
Medium	Medium	Medium/Low	Medium/Low
Evolutionary	Evolutionary/ Stable	Evolutionary/ Stable	Evolutionary/ Stable
High/Medium	High/Medium	High	Medium/Low
Evolutionary/	Evolutionary/	Stable/	Stable/
Stable	Stable	Evolutionary	Evolutionary
High	High	High	High
Medium/High	Medium/High	Medium	Low/Medium
Medium/High	Medium/High	Low	Low
Medium	High	Medium	Low/Medium
Medium	High	Medium	Low/Medium
High	High	High	High
Low	Medium	Medium	Medium
High	Medium	Medium	Medium
Medium/High	Medium/High	Medium/High	Medium/High
Yes	Yes	Yes	Yes
Yes	Yes	Yes	Yes
Yes	Yes	Yes	Yes
Many repetitive operations	Many repetitive operations	Number of operations for each	Number of operations for each
Little variability	Little variability	job highly variable	job highly variable

After the initial debugging phase and learning period, the overall performance of the Autotech line was very impressive. Despite the complexity and length of the manufacturing process, a cycle time of less than ten days was achieved.

Despite the excellent design concepts of the Autotech line, it experienced periods of deterioration in performance in three areas—throughput, inventory, and cycle time. For the first two years of its operation, the line was relatively lightly loaded and operating well below its designed capacity. Although the line experienced its share of process and equipment problems, these problems did not seriously detract from line performance, since the capacity of the line was not constrained.

After the first two years, there was a sudden surge in demand for the product, and the line capacity was tested for the first time. Due to the stress of high production schedules, serious process and equipment problems caused a stop in production and resulted in excessive work

Table 13–2
Definitions of Industry Classifications

	Classification
1. *Environment*	
a. *Degree of product/process change:* change in product/process from preceding generation	
More than 70%	Revolutionary
More than 10%, less than 70%	Evolutionary
Less than 10%	Stable
b. *Mix variability:* number of different part numbers	
More than 100	High
More than 50, less than 100	Medium
Less than 50	Low
c. *Stability:* frequency of stoppage in production due to process problems (lasting several hours or more)	
Less than monthly	High
Monthly	Medium
Weekly	Low
Daily	Very low
2. *Control Environment*	
a. *Mechanization:* individual operations which use machines	
More than 30%	Very high
More than 20%	High
Less than 20%, more than 10%	Medium
Less than 10%	Low
b. *Automation:* operations under mechanization and systemization[a]	
More than 30%	Very high
More than 20%	High
Less than 20%, more than 10%	Medium
Less than 10%	Low
c. *Computer control:* degree of computer systemization	
Data collection, monitor, guide, control, report	High
Data collection, monitor, guide, report	Medium
Data collection and report	Low
Computers not used	None
d. *Logistics control:* production (throughput) rate, line inventory, and cycle time data	
Very accurate real time automatic tracking with computers; product tracking at sector, operator, tool level	Very high
Accurate real time tracking with computer; product tracking at sector level or operation level	High
Accurate batch tracking with computers; product tracking at sector level or operation level	Medium
Manual recording without computers	Low
Product logistics data not recorded	None
3. *Cost structure for capital, labor, overhead and materials:* percentage of manufacturing cost	
More than 30%	Very high

Table 13–2   continued

	Classification
More than 20%	High
More than 10%, less than 20%	Medium
Less than 10%	Low

4. *Product structure:* relates to the product levels
    manufactured by the company in its own
    manufactured line; does not include purchased or
    subcontracted items

[a]*Systemization:* use of information handling systems to perform such functions as data collection by recording, monitoring by inquiry and alarm, guiding by providing alternatives, direct or indirect control.

queues. Because production was at a level close to the maximum capacity of the line, reducing these queues took a long time. The line inventory and cycle time continued to increase, and throughput declined considerably. Because of these circumstances the techniques outlined in chapter 8 were employed.

Each Autotech process operation had a planned production rate (throughput) and a planned cycle time. The expected inventory level is the product of these two numbers. By comparing these numbers with the actual throughput, inventory level, and cycle time performance for each operation, any chronic bottlenecks that existed could be identified.

Most of the operations in the Autotech line were automated. Only a few operations, including visual inspections and rework, were manual and required operators. Because this system was primarily automated, every effort was made to employ as few people as possible and where practical to share these people among the manual operations.

When the performance of the line was analyzed and compared to the plan, several bottlenecks were discovered. These bottlenecks occurred at one of the critical process steps as well as at visual inspection and rework. Once identified, the solution to these bottlenecks became obvious. Additional manpower at these steps was added. In less than a month, the line was again operating at its performance objectives. The cycle time and inventory levels had been reduced by more than 25 percent, and the product output had increased by almost 40 percent. This example demonstrates that the performance of a capital-intensive production line can be severely degraded by the lack of only a few operators. The additional expense for this addition of labor represented much less than a 1 percent increase in the cost of the product. The increased output and the decrease in cycle time and inventory levels far outweighed this minute cost increase. The productivity increase was spectacular.

One year later, the Autotech line was again stressed to its maximum capacity because of increased demand for new part numbers and higher production requirements. Again the cycle time and inventory showed sharp increases. Using the same techniques described earlier to characterize the performance of the line revealed that of the twenty-four sectors on this line, only four of them were responsible for more than one-half the queue time. In this case, however, the increase in cycle time and inventory levels was not due to a shortage of direct labor. The bottlenecks resulted from the softness or instability of two processes that were being performed at these sectors. Both of these processes had been the most recent innovations added to the line. They were still in the early learning period and were behaving unpredictably. Once the analysis of the data revealed the existence of these bottlenecks, much greater emphasis was applied to these processes. In addition, small increments of resources were added to these sectors to increase their capacity. As a result of these actions, the performance of the line was quickly restored to its rated levels.

Case 2: High Technology and a Revolutionary Product and Process

This case study describes how the productivity techniques discussed in this book can be applied to a high technology product that was introduced into manufacturing for the first time in U.S. industry. The product, an electronic assembly, consisted of several subassemblies, each of which was highly susceptible to manufacturing yield losses. Every subassembly is made up of twenty-four components, each of which was also experiencing different levels of yield losses. The complexity of this product was further compounded by the fact that it was to be manufactured with totally new processes consisting of more than 100 operations. Furthermore, these processes were carried out with a completely new and untested set of equipment.

This product is representative of a wide range of innovative high technology products that we classify as revolutionary. Many product, process, and equipment problems were to be expected during the introduction of a product with so much complexity and novelty. Using this product, manufactured by the Revol Corporation, we describe a number of manufacturing problems and how the application of our productivity techniques solved them. These problems can be classified in four categories:

1. The propagation of bottlenecks
2. Component repair and subassembly tests

3. Unique components and associated unique tools
4. Materials requirement planning (MRP) systems-run frequency

The Propagation of Bottlenecks

The Revol product is manufactured using many operations and processes that have never been practiced before in any technology. Most of the processes and equipment can be classified as new or soft. Even evolutionary technologies have some degree of softness in the early stages of production. But the type of product represented by Revol presents far-more difficulty in its introduction into manufacturing.

There seems to be a common characteristic for all revolutionary products during the early stages of production: the propagation of chronic bottlenecks from the beginning of the process to the end. The time and resource expended for the early manufacturing period is seldom sufficient to ensure that the product is manufacturable. The rush to institute this product into production forces short-cuts and compromises that often create major problems. The transition from laboratory development to high-volume manufacturing is a vital, and often neglected, phase of the entire product cycle. Making a few hundred operable parts in the laboratory is an essential but highly insufficient basis for judging that a product can be manufactured at a competitive cost with high reliability in a high-production environment. Even the pilot production of several thousand of a high technology product may be inadequate to verify the manufacturability of the product. There must be a thorough period of testing of the tools and processes to prove that they work together properly as production volumes increase. During this period, processes and tools may have to be modified and retested until the entire production system is brought under control, and until it can be proved that the product can be manufactured consistently with a high yield and high reliability.

Even with the most extensive period of stressing and debugging of a production line introducing a revolutionary product, there will never be enough time to do the job completely. Competitive pressures and financial realities may force the premature introduction of such a product into manufacturing.

The result of this premature introduction is the problem of bottleneck propagation. Because of the low level of learning, with the start of production, a bottleneck is usually formed at the beginning of the line. As each succeeding operation is stressed, a new bottleneck is formed at that operation. This phenomenon is exactly the problem that plagued the Revol lines.

The first serious trouble appeared in the first operation of the line making one of the components of the subassembly. A bottleneck appeared for a short period and was corrected. A new bottleneck appeared at the next operation and lasted for several months. Then a third operation, inspect and repair, became a bottleneck. All three of the major operations used in the manufacturing line for this component became chronic bottlenecks in a successive manner as the product flowed downstream.

A similar propagation of chronic bottlenecks occurred in the subassembly line. The first serious bottleneck problems occurred in the first two operations and were corrected rather quickly. But once the subassemblies arrived at the more difficult process operations later in the line, the work flow almost completely stopped. This operation remained a chronic bottleneck. After several months, a subsequent testing operation became the next bottleneck.

The Revol Corporation, in its zeal to manufacture a revolutionary product, undertook a risk by beginning production with inadequate proof of manufacturability. The result was the creation of several chronic bottlenecks that, one by one, were created as each successive process was stressed as production increased. All these bottlenecks lasted for several months. Two of the operations were far more serious than the others, however. These operations consisted of the most difficult process operations with the greatest degree of innovation and the least manufacturing experience. In other words, these processes were the softest and presented the greatest potential for extended bottlenecks.

Revol management realized that it had greatly underestimated the degree of learning that was still required before its personnel mastered the manufacturability of this product. Once management recognized this fact and identified the chronic bottlenecks that resulted from its underplanning, it allocated the additional resources needed to break them. The line balancing techniques discussed in this book played a major role in solving the Revol problems.

Component Repair and Subassembly Test

Manufacturing management usually underestimates the amount of rework and inspection required during the early manufacture of a new technology. Revol was no exception. During the early manufacturing of its product, the number of defects per component was extremely high. The only way management could cope with this high level was to inspect and rework the parts frequently during the production process. Because Revol had seriously underplanned its inspection and rework, major bottlenecks were created. Until management understood the problem, these bottlenecks continued unabated with a major impact on productivity. Once it recognized that these bottlenecks existed and where they were located, it acted decisively to remove them. In this case, it subcontracted these operations to a vendor. The additional expense was a very small fraction of the total manufacturing cost, but the improvement in productivity and reduction in product cost was dramatic.

The subassembly testing was performed by a tester connected to a computer. This tester identified each electrical defect by type and location. The computer analysis was verified by means of an analysis tool that used a display screen that magnified the image 100 times. A laser tool corrected the defects that were repairable. In addition to spotting individual defects, the inspection tools enabled engineers to monitor, diagnose, and correct problems that may have occurred throughout the manufacturing process.

The Revol subassembly test sector was plagued by two problems that are common to many test operations. First, because the test and inspection activities were monitored as a single entity, it was not possible to determine whether problems were due to inadequate test capacity or an insufficient number of engineers to perform diagnostics. Chapter 9, on cycle time, stressed the need to either break up multiple critical operations in a sector into several sectors or implement operational level tracking instead of sector-level tracking. Following this approach, Revol separated the testers from the diagnostics and quickly identified its trouble spot as the lack of engineers assigned to inspect, monitor, diagnose, and correct problems. It assigned additional engineers and immediately eliminated the bottleneck. This example demonstrates the importance of taking a microscopic view of a bottleneck to properly identify the true cause and the type of resource needed to eliminate it.

Another problem that is typical of a test sector is the excessive recycling of product within the test sector itself. Revol used a test analysis tool with high magnification to visually detect defects. If defects were found, a laser tool was used to correct the repairable defects on the assembly. The repaired subassembly was again sent to the tester for detecting any remaining defects. If additional defects were discovered, the assembly was again returned for inspection and repair. In fact, this cycle of testing, inspection, and repair was repeated several times. During the early life of the Revol product, subassemblies were often recycled four times or more and in some cases in excess of ten times. Obviously, this recycling consumed a great deal of test and diagnostic capacity. Once Revol recognized that this excessive cycling was occurring, it was relatively easy to show that those subassemblies that were recycled three times showed a high probability of having to be recycled indefinitely.

The type of recycling problem discovered by Revol engineers is not uncommon. Such a problem should be analyzed to determine the point of diminishing returns for this type of recycling activity. In the case of the Revol example, there was no value in repairing the subassembly after three times. Continued fruitless recycling after that point would result in a chronic bottleneck. Eliminating the bottleneck at Revol greatly increased the effective capacity of these sectors by removing the product that had little likelihood of passing the test sector successfully.

Unique Components and Associated Unique Tools

The Revol subassembly consisted of twenty-four different components, each of which experienced different levels of manufacturing yield losses. The manufacturing process for producing these components was extremely complex, and this complexity presented many opportunities for bottlenecks to appear.

The manufacturing of the Revol subassembly could not be started unless all twenty-four components were available. A comparable problem would exist if a large commercial jet airplane were complete with the exception of one critical bolt holding one of the four engines in place: the plane could not be flown safely. In the case of the Revol product, if enough production capacity existed to make twenty-three components, there should be enough capacity to make the twenty-fourth. The Revol subassembly, however, experienced two problems that prevented manufacture of complete sets of the twenty-four components that formed the completed subassemblies.

Even though all of the components in the subassembly looked alike physically, they performed different functions and varied in complexity. For example, component A performed the most comprehensive electrical functions and was by far the most complex in its physical structure. During the early stages of manufacturing, the yield for this component was less than 10 percent. For every 100 of component A started in manufacturing, only 10 passed the final inspection step at the end of the process. The remaining 90 were scrapped somewhere in the manufacturing line. Of course, Revol engineers were aware of the relative difficulty of manufacturing component A but greatly underestimated that difficulty. They planned yields in the range of 50 percent but actually experienced yields of only 10 percent. Furthermore, the variability of yield by production lot was great.

Component B, a power component that distributed voltage to other components, was also very complex. Underplanning of the resource to build these components added to Revol's problems. The impact of the shortages of both components A and B on the production of Revol subassemblies was nothing short of catastrophic. Even though the total volume of components produced by the component production line met and often exceeded the planned output, it was not possible to make enough subassemblies. The line balancing techniques discussed in chapter 8 could not identify this problem easily because no individual sector in the line behaved as a chronic bottleneck. Each sector met its planned daily throughput rate, yet the release of subassemblies into the subassembly line was less than one-third the planned level. Revol faced a classic production control dilemma. Manufacturing was producing hundreds of thousands of components and meeting the required volume, but it was not producing them to the required mix of products. The total number or parts produced met or exceeded the planned targets, but the individual part numbers were not produced in the correct quantities.

Once Revol engineers determined that yields of component A and B were much lower than they had planned, they began to use the actual performance in their planning. The Revol material requirements planning system began to reflect the real yield numbers for these complex components. Although these troublesome components continued to cause shortages, the problems were greatly minimized by building inventory buffers when capacity permitted.

Another problem that aggravated the production of these two components was the shortage of unique tools required in each of their manufacturing processes. Not only was there a unique tool for each component type, but the life of each tool was limited. The number of times each tool can be used before it is discarded was called its *pass factor*. The pass factor for a unique tool at Revol also varied considerably and depended on the complexity of the individual component for which the tool was used.

Revol engineers discovered that the unique tool used for component A was experiencing pass factors considerably below the factor in the production plan. Even though the planned yield of the component A had been lowered to the actual experienced value, and sufficient releases of the component had been made to the line, the actual production of component A was now being constrained because there were not enough unique tools to carry out the process. The production line making these unique tools was itself severely strained. Furthermore, it was not easy to convince management of the need for producing additional unique tools for component A.

Why would the department that had the responsibility for making the unique tools be reluctant to increase their production? The management believed that it was doing its job well: it had a plan, and it was meeting its plan. The plan called for the production of a certain number of tools, and the management delivered these tools in sufficient quantities, on schedule. Why should it deliver more? At Revol the unique tool was part of a total manufacturing system. The system consisted of the manufacture of the electronic assembly, the subassembly, the components required for the subassembly, and the processes and tools, unique or otherwise, required to build all of the pieces of the assembly. The head of the operation making the unique tool must realize that he is a critical element of the total system. Unless additional unique tools for the critical components were manufactured on short notice, the production of these components would be seriously affected.

Eventually, Revol put its act together. A combination of the right yield planning for components *A* and *B* and the increase in production of the proper level of unique tools alleviated the component part type mix problem. The number of Revol subassemblies that could now be released was tripled. This represented a 200 percent increase in productivity.

Materials Requirement Planning

The preceding section discussed the shortage of critical components of the Revol subassembly. Anyone acquainted with materials requirement planning systems (MRP) would agree that these shortages should never have occurred if a proper system had been implemented. What constitutes a proper MRP system? Did Revol have one?

Revol had installed a sophisticated MRP system that regenerated job priorities and unique part requirements, called part numbers, on a monthly basis. The monthly schedule was adjusted manually on a daily basis depending on the losses in the component and subassembly lines. During the first two years Revol produced seventy-five different subassembly part numbers, each of which had twenty-four different components. All the component types, as well as the subassembly part numbers, were subject to very different manufacturing losses. This dynamic and constrained manufacturing environment made it difficult for Revol to keep up with job priorities and subassembly releases to production. Revol remedied this problem by instituting a daily MRP system. This system was far more effective in reacting to the daily component and subassembly losses as well as the varying production delays that resulted from new product and processes and equipment. Later, when production capacity was better able to meet the demand, component inventory on difficult part numbers was built in order to serve as a buffer for the variation in manufacturing losses.

Two lessons can be learned from Revol's experience. First, the production of a revolutionary high technology product demands at least a daily computer MRP system to react to yield and cycle time variations to prevent serious shortages. Second, the planning parameters used in the system must reflect actual, not fictitious, production conditions. The MRP system initially installed by Revol was ineffective because the planning numbers used were very optimistic. The planned yield for component *A* was 50 percent compared to an actual yield of 10 percent. Furthermore, the yield varied greatly from day to day.

On many occasions, jobs for certain problem component types were totally scrapped because of manufacturing defects. After much painstaking data gathering and analysis it was discovered that the probability of losing more than two consecutive jobs for the same part type was extremely low. As a result, Revol substantially reduced the loss of jobs by staggering the jobs for the same part numbers and reduced the quantity per job for difficult types.

Revol used the data gathering techniques described in this book. They increased the frequency of running their MRP system to at least once a day and used realistic planning parameters. As a result, they resolved the extremely difficult production problems in their lines. The productivity gains varied from 25 to 30 percent to over 200 percent during the implementation of the strategies discussed in this case study.

Case 3: Evolutionary High Technology Environment

High technology products and processes often undergo a highly unstable period for three to five years after they are introduced into production. After this phase these products pass through a period of less instability, possibly for several years, until they reach a state of reasonable stability for the remainder of their life. Evtech Company was manufacturing high technology products that were characterized by an evolutionary process. The electrical test yields were in the range of 25 to 60 percent and the planned level of rework was less than 10 percent. Most high technology manufacturing, especially in the semiconductor industry, is characterized by this kind of evolutionary product and process environment with these levels of yield and rework.

Evtech manufactured its principle product on two lines consisting of approximately sixty sectors. The first line produced partially processed product that was later used to fabricate a wide variety of part numbers in the second manufacturing line. The second manufacturing line, called the custom line, was performing at a monthly average of approximately 50 to 60 percent of its rated capacity. This condition had existed for an extended period, even though in some weeks the production achieved as high as 90 percent of the rated capacity. Because of concern for the wide fluctuation in weekly line performance—from 20 to 90 percent of the rated capacity—management followed several traditional approaches to improve the performance of the custom line.

As a result of using several normal methods of increasing productivity in a constrained factory, management succeeded in achieving some immediate but temporary results. These methods included asking people to work harder, introducing quality circles, and using a higher level of overtime, weekends, and additional shifts. Even a "flying squad" consisting of a team of highly skilled and versatile workers had been mobilized to move a bubble of work-in-process inventory through the line.

Management review meetings were scheduled on a daily basis, at the beginning of the day shift, to discuss the previous day's performance. Management representatives attended from the major production organizations, including manufacturing, production control, manufacturing engineering, industrial engineering, equipment engineering, maintenance, and quality control. Although the purpose of these meetings was to exchange ideas on increasing production, they often generated a great deal of finger-pointing and mutual criticism. Production control was blamed for poor planning and scheduling, manufacturing for inept labor performance and inefficient expediting. Equipment engineering was castigated for inferior equipment design and low availability and serviceability. Quality control was accused of writing unnecessarily tight specifications. Maintenance was blamed for taking too long to make repairs. Many management executives will recognize this familiar unfolding of events. The course of action taken by the management of the custom line is traditional and commonplace.

After a lengthy period of marginal improvements in the custom line, manufacturing management became convinced that it needed to focus on chronic bottlenecks. The custom line consisted of twenty-seven sectors of which at least twenty had been bottlenecks at one time or another. These bottlenecks were detected by comparing weekly performance with the rated capacity. Using the techniques outlined in chapter 8 on line balancing management identified five chronic bottleneck sectors. These sectors were producing at an average of 50 to 60 percent of their rated capacity for at least four out of six consecutive weeks. The average work-in-process inventory at these sectors varied from approximately 1.5 to 3.0 times the planned value. Even though more than twenty of the twenty-seven sectors had been temporary bottlenecks, only five of the twenty-seven sectors were chronic bottlenecks.

Once the management system of the custom line identified the five chronic bottleneck sectors, it took some very specific long-term actions as opposed to the short-term approach it had previously followed in the daily management review meetings. First, it obtained unanimous agreement that regardless of the nature of the problems that afflicted these five chronic bottlenecks and who was responsible for their solution, it was absolutely necessary to increase their capacity if long-term gains in production were to be achieved. Direct workers were moved permanently into these five chronic bottleneck sectors. Also, some of the most skilled workers, including maintenance personnel and process and equipment engineers, were immediately moved to these sectors from less critical operations and areas of surplus manpower. The reallocation of direct workers from noncritical to chronic bottleneck sectors is generally one of the first and most effective steps in balancing a line. Even if most of the line is suffering from chronic bottlenecks, it may be worthwhile to move direct workers from less critical to more critical chronic bottleneck sectors. After all, the purpose is to maximize the total production of the entire manufacturing line.

At the end of the first week, these five bottlenecks were reduced to four, by the second week only one remained, and at the end of the third week all the chronic bottlenecks had completely disappeared. The throughput of the five chronic bottlenecks had been increased by 75 percent to more than 100 percent. Line work-in-process inventory and cycle time had both been reduced by almost 40 percent.

A later analysis of this impressive improvement in line performance revealed that several major actions were responsible. Three problem tools were repaired by expert maintenance and equipment engineering help. An extra piece of equipment scheduled for a later delivery was expedited. Manufacturing management and process engineers, recognizing the excessive level of rework, assigned extra equipment (obtained from noncritical sectors) and direct workers. The sharp management focus on these five bottleneck sectors had paid off handsome dividends.

Case 4: General Large-Scale Industries

The Japanese post–World War II industrial record has been impressive. Japan's market domination extends over a wide spectrum of industries—steel, cameras, watches, motorcycles, optics, home appliances, electrical equipment, consumer electronics, textiles, precision equipment. In several other areas, the Japanese lead had also become substantial. When two major industries, automobiles and office products, were targeted by the Japanese for future market domination, the management at GLSI Corporation decided to pursue an aggressive productivity program.

In the mid-1970s GLSI marketed consumer and industrial products. These markets were responsible for its position in the top 100 U.S. companies with the largest annual sales, revenues, and profits. The number of models, colors, optional equipment, features, and accessories offered by GLSI had continued to increase and changed annually. In some cases, it changed models twice a year. The result was an explosion in the number of parts and products that needed to be produced, controlled, and managed. Management had foreseen the need to control literally hundreds of thousands of parts and had already implemented an MRP (material requirement planning) system. This integrated system scheduled many of the GLSI manufacturing locations, as well as several of its vendors. It extended control over many other GLSI functions, including purchasing, warehousing, finance, engineering, and marketing.

The MRP system at GLSI had already achieved many of the benefits attributed to such computer-oriented production information and control systems. Among the business advantages were a more accurate bill of materials, information, and control of engineering changes, improved inventory control, reduced work-in-process, more valid order priorities and schedules, and better control of material receipts and movements. The list of accomplishments over the previous decade had indeed been impressive.

In addition to the advantages of MRP, GLSI management was quick to realize the potential benefits of computers, automation, robotics, and electronics (CARE). After all, these evolutionary advances of the 1960s were advertised to be the cure for the ills of industry in the 1970s and beyond.

GLSI introduced robots in many of the welding, painting, machine loading, assembly die casting, and palletization operations, and these robots improved quality, appearance, uniformity, repeatability, and reliability. Increased automation was implemented to varying degrees, especially in assembly and test operations.

GLSI also pursued an aggressive policy of implementing electronic products and additional computer control in many of its manufacturing operations. A variety of magnetic and optical parts identification and tracking aids were introduced as elements of an overall sensor-based production control system. This approach improved the level of logistics data accuracy. Verification of part identity through noncontact bar code reading was used to ensure the proper assembly of components. Time lost in locating parts was reduced substantially.

Electronics and computers also were implemented to assist in equipment maintenance, equipment monitoring, and dispatching repairmen. By monitoring the status of critical equipment and dispatching maintenance personnel promptly on the failure of equipment, down-time was reduced. The monitoring of key equipment operating characteristics permitted preventive maintenance to be properly scheduled, thus avoiding costly breakdowns. GLSI management believed that its measures reduced manufacturing costs by more than 10 percent.

GLSI was very aggressive in promoting its productivity programs. It adopted many well-known techniques such as MRP and CARE. Furthermore, it implemented many other programs that are beyond the scope of this case study. The consciousness of the effect of productivity on cost and competitiveness was high at GLSI, and it was aggressive in taking decisive actions. But what were the results? Manufacturing costs were reduced by over 10 percent, a modest although valuable improvement. Furthermore, the inventory turnover ratio, the ratio of cost of goods sold to the average inventory, increased from 6 in the mid-1970s to more than 8. As a result of all of the programs GLSI energetically promoted, overall productivity improved. But the competition also improved, and to a much greater degree. A foreign competitor, the subject of the category 5 case study, achieved an inventory turnover ratio of approximately 70.

Case 5: Repetitive Operations with Limited Variability

The Repop Corporation's management had a formidable challenge: its goal was to become the most efficient manufacturer in the world. As if that were not challenge enough, it had to cope with a serious limitation: it operated in a country with little or no sources of energy and raw materials and was severely limited in space.

Repop's foreign competitors, of which GLSI (category 4) was one, offered the consumer a wide variety of models, colors, optional equipment, features, and accessories. These competitors placed great emphasis on comfort and styling features that were attractive to consumers.

Repop adopted a different strategy. Of course, it wanted to sell its customers attractive and comfortable products. But it placed a high priority on quality and energy efficiency, characteristics that were important not only to the domestic market but to the foreign consumer as well.

In order to become the lowest-cost manufacturer, Repop adopted two major strategies. First, unlike GLSI, it carefully limited the number of its products and parts by offering a limited number of consumer options. Second, it developed a manufacturing system that was designed to identify all bottlenecks and force their immediate resolution by a systematic process of reducing inventory. Its approach was to use a method that continuously highlighted critical manufacturing bottleneck problems, even at the expense of temporarily stopping the entire manufacturing line.

Repop management instituted a system commonly known as just-in-time (JIT). To create the right manufacturing environment for this system, it limited the product line so that most of the parts could be repetitively manufactured. It chose vendors that were physically located close to its manufacturing facilities. To create further stability in the production process, it froze production schedules for a month at a time. Repop allowed only small incremental changes.

The next tactical step taken by Repop was perhaps the most important and radical. The management placed responsibility for shop floor production control and productivity improvement directly on the workers and the first-line supervisors. In order to successfully assign the responsibilities to these people, Repop developed an attitude of close cooperation and mutual trust between the work force and the management. Finally, management repeatedly emphasized the importance of taking any actions that would aid the continual flow of parts, even if it meant temporarily stopping the production line.

Repop's JIT system was initially a manual one. Computers were used only to develop the master assembly schedule. The assembly schedule mix was to provide an even and consistent flow of parts through all of the work centers, both inside the plant and at the vendors. Although the assembly schedule was established with computers, material flow and production control were carried out manually. Repop's JIT system operated essentially as a pull system: parts were drawn from feeding work centers that produced parts in the same quantities that were withdrawn by the assembly line. The production usually required the consumption of parts produced by the previous work center in the supply chain, which triggered the second work center to replace only those parts that were used by the first work center. This process repeated itself down the entire manufacturing supply chain. Each work center was closely linked to the work centers that it fed and to the work center that supplied its parts. If a stoppage or pause occurred in any operation, in a short period of time all work centers and the assembly line came to a halt for lack of work.

Repop used JIT as a productivity improvement system by forcing the recognition and resolution of bottlenecks. When the plant became essentially balanced with no critical shortages and no excessive overtime, management actually withdrew inventory from the production floor. By withdrawing this inventory, one of the production resources became a constraint on the total output of the system. The bottleneck manifested itself by either having to work large amounts of overtime or by producing insufficient parts to keep the next work center or the assembly line in operation. Management was satisfied that now it had identified the operation that was limiting the output of the total system and would also limit further inventory reduction. With this valuable knowledge, it could now concentrate on solving the problem revealed by these actions.

Solutions could be achieved in many ways, but Repop management concentrated on the lowest-cost alternative. If labor was a constraint, additional workers would be cross-trained to supplement the workers currently at that operation. If a machine was a constraint, management focused on unused machine hours to determine how more capacity could be made available. It might reduce setup times or improve preventive maintenance to increase productive hours. If inconsistent quality caused problems, it was remedied. As a last resort, management would even add an additional piece of equipment if other measures were not effective. Whatever the cause, the necessary steps were always taken to remove the bottleneck. These actions increased the total output and further reduced inventory levels.

Once a steady state condition was reestablished, additional inventory was again withdrawn from production until the next bottleneck appeared. This procedure, followed by Repop for many years, resulted in extremely high and dependable quality, a flexible work force, excellent preventive maintenance, and very quick setups. These results were not goals in themselves. They were the natural result of the continuous action they took to remove bottlenecks from their manufacturing plants.

JIT systems of the type installed by Repop have been used with great success by many Japanese companies and are being considered seriously by several U.S. companies. The success of Repop's system can be seen from its improved inventory ratio. Starting from a value just below 40 in the mid-1960s, Repop's inventory ratio today is greater than 70. This performance is especially spectacular when compared to the GLSI's present inventory turnover of 8.

Despite the success of Repop and many other companies in the use of JIT, the system contains some serious limitations. JIT is applicable only in repetitive manufacturing environments. Even in repetitive situations, it must be possible to freeze the assembly schedule for some period of time. JIT works best when vendors are located near the base manufacturing facility. Furthermore, the lines must be standardized, have a limited number of options, and have a stable product mix. Too high a mix requires too many temporary work stoppages and produces a lack of focus on critical problem areas. Too many stoppages, even those of a short duration, can have a serious negative effect on productivity.

Another factor makes JIT extremely difficult to institute successfully: JIT requires a great deal of commitment by and support and assistance from the workers and the first-line supervision to succeed. Even in Japan, where there is a great commitment to group rather than individual goals, JIT has not always worked successfully. Nevertheless, just-in-time systems, under the right circumstances of product mix and stability and with the good management and worker attitudes, can be very profitable.

Case 6: Medium-Scale Industrial Environment

The MSI Corporation performance record was impressive. Management at MSI was able to cope with the two economic recessions of the early and mid-1970s rather well. Beginning with the second quarter of 1976, the demand for MSI products continued to grow steadily and for more than two years the company met the challenge. At first, the normal two-shift manufacturing schedule was subjected to heavy overtime, followed by the introduction of a partial third shift and occasional weekend work. Gradually a full third shift was instituted, and production was carried out on a three-shift, seven-day basis.

Six months after it converted to twenty-one shifts a week, MSI management discovered that it was producing less work in the fifth and sixth month than in each of the first four months. Production decreased by a staggering 20 percent from its peak. Cycle time and inventory had each grown by about 33 percent during the same period that throughput had fallen by 20 percent. Mass confusion and lack of control reigned on the manufacturing floor.

The situation that developed at MSI is a problem common to many manufacturers when a production facility is continually or rapidly stressed. The typical manufacturing superintendent's policy is to keep all workers and machines fully busy, particularly in the face of rising schedules. An overzealous production control manager at MSI continued to increase releases into the manufacturing line in response to an ever-increasing demand: no self-respecting production control manager wants to be accused of incompetence by failing to release sufficient orders into the line.

The MSI manufacturing superintendent and production control manager agreed that the more work that was released into the line, the greater would be the pressure on the workers to produce more. After all, they reasoned, a third shift of work and weekends had been scheduled, and workers could easily understand the need to increase production.

What actually occurred on the manufacturing floor was very different from what was anticipated by the manufacturing superintendent and production control manager. Prior to a drop off in production in the fifth and sixth month of the twenty-one shifts a week operation, the output of the facility had actually surged in the third and fourth months. In the face of this surge, the performance in the fifth and sixth months seemed rather puzzling. The release of orders into the manufacturing line had been suddenly increased in the third and fourth months. Because the average cycle time for a job was in excess of two months, the effect of this escalation had not been felt until the fifth and sixth months. The increase in releases had resulted in large queues, particularly in the front end of the line. Because the cycle time and inventory increased by 33 percent, it became necessary to drastically increase the number of jobs being prioritized.

The floor logistics system of the MSI Corporation was unable to handle the large volume of work-in-process inventory. The storage and floor space to handle such a large number of jobs was insufficient. Moreover the paperwork and tracking cards accompanying the jobs were lost amid the confusion that now was rampant in many work centers. The department technician spent an excessive amount of time locating and prioritizing jobs. Due to the apparent inability of the department technicians to handle the floor logistics, manufacturing and production control management descended on the floor to determine the reasons for the problem.

Even senior management spent time assisting in locating, prioritizing, and moving "hot jobs," under customer pressure, when production was constrained, a direct involvement that is not unusual for higher management to take in attempting to solve production problems. Despite its involvement, however, there was little improvement.

After three months, the manufacturing management asked a logistics expert from another company location to study MSI's production problems. He suggested a rather bold approach. Because the level of confusion on the factory floor had reached almost frenzied proportions, why not, he suggested, simply limit the input of orders into the line? At first, this unconventional recommendation was greeted with some incredulity. MSI manufacturing management had always prided itself for its commitment to do everything within its power to meet production as long as a demand existed for its products. Actually limiting releases into the line didn't seem consistent with these objectives.

Nevertheless, after initially resisting this suggestion, management agreed to try the suggestion of the logistics expert. Accordingly, no jobs were released into the line for a three-week period. After two weeks elapsed, order began to be restored on the factory floor. At the end of the third week, throughput began to increase after a decline of five successive months. Starting with the fourth week jobs were gradually reintroduced into the line at a steadily increasing rate. At no time was the rate of introduction of new jobs into the line allowed to exceed the rate of jobs completed. Within two months of this controlled mode of job introduction, the throughput of the line not only reached its previous peak but surpassed it by an additional 25 percent. A cycle time improvement of 20 percent was also achieved during the same time period.

Steps such as stopping the release of new jobs into the manufacturing line as well as controlling the rate of introduction of new jobs can be a simple but very powerful means of improving manufacturing line performance.

Case 7: Small-Scale Industrial Environment

The control environment described in this case study is somewhat outmoded, particularly when compared to the first five case studies. Nevertheless, it is typical of many small industries that do not make it to the Fortune 500.

The SSI Corporation was a small-scale enterprise best characterized as a job shop operation. SSI processed approximately 100 jobs each day. Each job required twenty to fifty batches of parts, and the number of part numbers being managed at any given time occasionally exceeded 25,000. The manual scheduling of this shop was often a nightmare.

The basic philosophy under which the management team operated was that if the men and machines were kept busy, the shop would automatically produce to its maximum. The inventory turnover of the SSI job shop ranged between 2 and 3. As with other job shops of its kind, the inventory turnover was low due to long lead times. Large work-in-process inventory queues were commonplace and were considered necessary for efficient utilization of men and machines.

The number and type of operations required for the different jobs was highly variable. There was a reasonable amount of equipment mechanization. Except for five tools, the equipment was not physically linked together. This physical decoupling of the line had resulted in numerous large queues throughout the job shop.

Computer control of the job shop was restricted to implementation of the typical files used in materials requirement planning systems such as bill of material, routing, open order, work center, and so forth. The work-in-process inventory was manually tracked using a card tracking system, and overall logistics control was essentially manual. Jobs were released into the manufacturing floor using a computer system, but subsequently logistics control of the jobs was manual.

The SSI approach to production control was typical of the majority of the job shops in the United States that use either totally manual or a computerized manual production control system to manage productivity in their operation. The SSI foreman was in charge of production control. Every morning he summoned the department technicians from each work center. The foreman would review, with the appropriate department technician, jobs queued up at his work center using the tracking cards for each job. At each work center, the jobs would be selected according to a specific priority criteria. Like many other job shops, the SSI foreman had tried a wide variety of priority criteria, which included

First in, first out (commonly known as FIFO)

Due date sequence (earliest delivery date first)

Minimum (shortest) manufacturing time

Maximum (longest) manufacturing time

Most important customers (based on profit)

Priorities dictated by upper management

Priorities dictated by sales people

Priority algorithms

The priority algorithm that had seemed to work best for SSI was a ratio of the difference between today's date and the due date to the estimated remaining cycle time. Expressed mathematically,

$$\text{job priority ratio} = \frac{\text{today's date} - \text{due date}}{\text{estimated remaining cycle time}}$$

The jobs were then sequenced starting with the largest positive job priority ratio to the largest negative job priority ratio. Even though a priority criteria was agreed on, job priorities were constantly revised, generally based on orders from above.

The manual production control system that SSI had implemented served it well for many years. When the volume of jobs was small, the foreman could easily prioritize and schedule them. As the operation grew, however, the number of combinations of jobs and schedules to consider exploded. Along with the realities of any manufacturing operation— such as equipment breakdown, variation in human skills, performance, absenteeism, material shortages, and so forth—the scheduling and prioritization of jobs became a nightmare. Business growth had resulted in confusion.

The average turn-around time for jobs of similar complexity continued to increase and more than doubled in less than six months. At this stage some of the methods described in this book were employed in a very simple and rudimentary manner. As a first step, the foreman walked through the entire job shop before the beginning of each shift. At each major work center, he manually recorded the average number of orders actively worked, as well as the number of orders waiting in the queue. Because SSI had less than two dozen work centers, this process took less than an hour to complete. The ratio of the number of orders waiting in the queue to the number of orders being actively worked in a work center is a good first approximation of the degree of congestion in that work center: the higher the ratio, the worse the condition in that bottleneck. By simply developing these ratios and ranking them in descending sequence, the foreman was able to rapidly identify the bottlenecks in his job shop. The foreman also discovered that four to six work centers were far more critical from the standpoint of production output than the remaining twenty. The next step, of course, was to allocate the necessary people and machines to alleviate the bottlenecks in the order of priority.

This straightforward technique resulted in an improvement of almost 15 percent throughput and a reduction in inventory of approximately 20 percent in a period of about two months. This experience clearly demonstrates that even in the absence of precise logistics and job tracking data, it is possible to alleviate bottlenecks and effect substantial productivity improvements. Also noteworthy is that instead of relying on conventional industrial engineering techniques to identify constrained work centers, the foreman simply observed the bottom line effect of the interaction that actually occurred on the floor. It didn't matter who was responsible for the congestion at the work centers. Far more important was that some work centers were more seriously congested than others. Unless these bottlenecks were removed, allocating resources elsewhere would not substantially increase the total output of the job shop.

By observing critical work centers and those with excess capacity for the day, the foreman simply moved skilled workers to where they were critically needed from where the need was less urgent. This obvious measure helped provide temporary capacity for critical work centers. This approach was in sharp contrast to the previous method where jobs were prioritized at each work center by the foreman and the department technician, no matter what the relative gravity of congestion at that work center. The new approach simply considered the total state of the job shop before a single job was prioritized and prior to the assignment of any workers to specific jobs. Of course, had the foreman used a precise logistics and job tracking system to identify chronic bottlenecks, he would have been able to make far more productive long-term decisions, such as hiring more workers and installing additional equipment where necessary.

14
Epilogue: The Seven Principles of U.S. Productivity

The road to productivity, like the road to hell, is paved with good intentions. U.S. industry is heavily investing in brains and capital to increase productivity, reduce costs, and improve its world competitive position. We are innovating, automating, computerizing, roboticizing, and measuring at an accelerating rate. Yet the overall effect of these actions on our nation's productivity has so far been relatively insignificant. U.S. world productivity leadership, which began to decline one or two decades ago, continues to erode. The standard of living of U.S. workers does not improve. The utilization of U.S. production capacity remains shockingly low.

The reasons for this state of affairs are intensely and continuously debated. Panaceas are advanced in abundance: more capital investment, lower corporate taxes, higher import tariffs, organized labor concessions, liberal antipollution laws, increased automation, and even adoption of widely advertised Japanese practices.

Despite well-intentioned and costly efforts to fight the battle of productivity, and in spite of the voluminous rhetoric on the subject, the indicators of U.S. progress, or lack of it, continue to alarm. Recently, Japan has moved new technologies from the research laboratory to marketable products much faster than the best U.S.-managed corporations. This fact is the most important single reason for Japan's superior productivity performance. The inventory turnover ratio of U.S. manufacturing is one-half that of Japan, and U.S. productivity growth lags the leading six industrial nations of the West. Nonproductive time of U.S. manufacturing lines is greater than 90 percent and our production capacity is operating at less than 30 percent of the utilization of which it is capable.

Combine these last two statistics, the 90 percent nonproductive time and the 30 percent utilization of capacity, with a third fact: most of U.S. industry operates with direct labor less than 20 percent and usually less than 10 percent, of the cost of product. Where should our priorities lie? Obviously, we must concentrate on the areas of greatest leverage—not the measurement and replacement of direct labor, but on increased output, reduced nonproductive time, and increased utilization of capacity. But we are doing precisely the opposite. U.S. measurement systems concentrate on analyzing with the most sensitive methods the performance of direct labor, and we are spending vast sums of capital to replace them. Is it any surprise that these efforts have resulted in only limited success?

What can we do about productivity? We can do plenty. The tools are available; they can be used with powerful leverage if we know how to use them, and above all, where to use them. The techniques presented in this book can be summarized in seven principles, as shown in figure 14–1. If U.S. industry follows these principles, it can make major advances in its drive for increased productivity and a healthier economy.

1. Accelerate the Movement of Products from the Laboratory to the Marketplace

Radically accelerate the movement of products from the research laboratory to the marketplace. Place a far greater emphasis on the production engineering necessary to make products manufacturable. Furthermore, change management techniques and develop a formidable partnership among research, development, production engineering, manufacturing, and marketing to make the transition from invention to the consumer as quickly and effectively as possible.

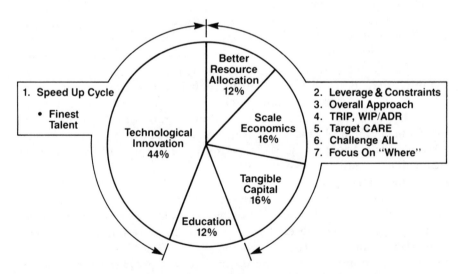

Figure 14–1. Recommendations for Increasing U.S. Productivity

2. Find Your Major Areas of Leverage and Constraints

Determine those areas that have the greatest effect in preventing you from moving your completed product out of the plant to the customer. Then identify your areas of greatest leverage. These are the areas where the greatest emphasis can yield the greatest results. Any management that intimately knows its products and its financial structure can identify these areas.

3. Don't Use Piecemeal Productivity Improvements

The manufacture of any product, from the simplest to the most complex, consists of an overall system. This system includes labor, materials, tools, maintenance people, engineers, management, and even the building that houses all of these resources. The successful operation of this system depends on a symbiotic relationship among all of these parts. Don't concentrate on one element of the system to the exclusion of the others, and don't concentrate on each element independently from the others: the system will either not work or will operate far below its capabilities.

4. Use Accurate Information to Measure Performance

Don't use assumptions: use actual numbers. Upper management, like every one else, likes to hear only good news; lower management likes to deliver only good news. Planning a factory with only happy assumptions on throughput, yield, tooling utilization, and labor productivity will, like a few extra drinks on New Year's Eve, result in a great deal of good cheer. Unfortunately, the good cheer will be brief. Not only will the reality eventually be discovered, but the plant will not operate according to these rosy predictions. What is worse, management will have difficulty knowing what actions to take to bring order out of the chaos. Management must constantly monitor actual performance and base its decisions and actions on realism, not mythical objectives.

5. Challenge Current Measurement Systems

Realize that the means of measuring performance today and in the future may be totally different from those of the past. Times have changed and are still changing. Don't cling to old fashioned methods just because you are comfortable with them because comfort may actually turn to failure. A preoccupation in accounting and industrial engineering with the measurement of direct labor distorts management's ability to find the major areas of leverage in its business. It prevents it from taking the actions that will yield major productivity improvements.

6. Carefully Target Powerful Productivity Tools

CARE can have an enormous impact on productivity if used strategically in the right places. Improperly used, computers, automation, robotics, and electronics are costly, complex, and actually counterproductive. They can create the illusion that we in U.S. industry are boldly attacking productivity. Yet the results of the recent past casts great doubt on whether this boldness has yielded any significant overall productivity gain. On the other hand, applying these tools to the right places, the areas having the greatest leverage, can be of great benefit. Be thoughtful about their application: indiscriminate application can be wasteful and counterproductive; thoughtful use can be of major importance.

7. Apply Direct Labor Strategically

Reducing direct labor under the guise of cost reduction can have serious negative consequences for the operation and effectiveness of the total manufacturing system. But the strategic infusion of direct labor, even small numbers at critical points of constraint, can yield powerful results and can greatly increase productivity. *Labor* is not a four-letter word; it is a major partner in the total manufacturing system. Of course, every operation engaged in manufacturing or a service can afford only the least number of people it needs to perform effectively; yet that number must be determined very carefully. That effectiveness may be greatly enhanced, not by reducing but by adding labor in high leverage areas.

No magic potion will cure all the ills of U.S. industry. These seven principles, however, if followed, can result in major productivity gains. In many circumstances, the gains can be dramatic. But it would be irresponsible to claim that these principles, by themselves, provide the magic elixir to solve all U.S. productivity problems.

A well-managed operation, a soundly designed product, a management team that knows its business and its products, a highly motivated work force, and a strong technical foundation are all prerequisites to success in achieving low-cost and high productivity. These elements are mandatory in the highly competitive world of products of increasing complexity and sophistication. The business that possesses the management, administrative, and technical strengths equal to the task of competing in this world will, of course, stand the best chance of survival and success.

We believe that a company with such a strong foundation can apply these seven principles with extraordinary success. Furthermore, we believe that these principles, when applied broadly throughout U.S. industry, can lead to major increases in total industrial productivity. We can get back into the race again and win.

Notes

Chapter 1
Introduction

1. U.S. Bureau of Labor Statistics. See *Monthly Labor Review*, 1968–1981; *Handbook of Labor Statistics*, annual, 1980, 1981; "The U.S. Productivity Crisis," *Newsweek*, September 8, 1980, p. 82; Council on Wage and Price Stability, *Report on Productivity* (Washington, D.C.: Executive Office of the President, 1979).

Chapter 2
Productivity and the Chief Executive

1. Thomas J. Peters and Robert H. Waterman, Jr., *In Search of Excellence: Lessons from America's Best-Run Companies* (New York: Harper & Row, 1982).
2. Ken Blanchard and Spencer Johnson, *The One Minute Manager* (New York: William Morrow, 1982).
3. John Naisbitt, *Megatrends*, (New York: Warner Books, 1982); Richard Schonberger, *Japanese Manufacturing Techniques* (New York: The Free Press, 1982); Philip Crosby, *Quality is Free* (New York: Mentor, 1980).
4. "Will Money Managers Wreck the Economy?", *Business Week*, Aug. 13, 1984, pp. 86, 87.
5. Ibid, p. 88.
6. Susan Fraker, "High-Speed Management for the High-Tech Age," *Fortune*, March 5, 1984, p. 62.
7. Robert H. Hayes and William J. Abernathy, "Managing Our Way to Economic Decline," *Harvard Business Review*, July-Aug. 1980, p. 25.
8. John Mayo, "Process Design as Important as Product Design," *Wall Street Journal*, Oct. 29, 1984, p. 32.
9. *Business Week*, July 16, 1984, p. 104.
10. Lester Thurow, as quoted in "Where Management Fails," *Newsweek*, Dec. 7, 1981, p. 78.

Chapter 3
Where is the Productivity Leverage?

1. *Webster's New Collegiate Dictionary* (Springfield, Mass.: G. & C. Merriam, 1977).

Chapter 4
Unlocking the Productivity Potential: What Is the Key?

1. Lester Thurow, as quoted in "A Non-Industrial Revolution," *Newsweek*, Jan. 9, 1984, p. 79.
2. John R. Opel, *Think*, Vol. 49, No. 2, March-April 1983, pp. 30, 32.
3. U.S. Bureau of Labor Statistics. See "America Rushes to High Tech for Growth," *Business Week*, March 28, 1983, p. 85.

Chapter 5
Innovation and Technology

1. Brookings Institution, Washington, D.C. (See fig. 2–2 in this book.)
2. D. Bruce Merrifield, "Forces of Change Affecting High Technology Industries," *National Journal*, Jan. 29, 1983, p. 255.
3. Robert H. Hayes and William J. Abernathy, "Managing Our Way to Economic Decline," *Harvard Business Review*, July-Aug. 1980, p. 12.
4. *Webster's New Collegiate Dictionary* (Springfield, Mass.: G. & C. Merriam, 1977).
5. *Webster's New Collegiate Dictionary* (Springfield, Mass.: G. & C. Merriam, 1977).

Chapter 6
Why Hasn't the U.S. Game Plan Worked?

1. *Business Week*, Dec. 24, 1984, p. 13.
2. Peter B. Hayhow, Paul Lingard, Paul Korzeniowski, and Joanne Kelleher, *PC Retailing (Newsweek* supplement), October 31, 1983.
3. Moshe Eliyahu Goldratt, as quoted in "Boosting Shop-Floor Productivity by Breaking All the Rules," *Business Week*, Nov. 26, 1984, p. 100.
4. Moshe Eliyahu Goldratt, as quoted in "Boosting Shop-Floor Productivity by Breaking All the Rules," *Business Week*, Nov. 26, 1984, p. 100.
5. Society of Manufacturing Engineers' and authors' own estimates.
6. Society of Manufacturing Engineers' and authors' own estimates.
7. K. Susnjara, *A Manager's Guide to Industrial Robots* (Shaker Heights, Ohio: Corinthian Press, 1982), p. 2.
8. "Machines That Think: They're Brewing a Revolution," *U.S. News and World Report*, Dec. 5, 1983, p. 60.
9. K. Susnjara, *A Manager's Guide to Industrial Robots* (Shaker Heights, Ohio: Corinthian Press, 1982), p. 33.
10. J. Stansell, "The Social Impact of Microprocessors," *New Scientist*, Oct. 12, 1978, pp. 104–106.

11. Based on several industry estimates, including John Naisbitt, *Megatrends* (New York: Warner Books, 1984), p. 31.

Chapter 7
Believe It or Not, We're Counterproductive

1. See Robert S. Kaplan, "Yesterday's Accounting Undermines Production," *Harvard Business Review,* July–Aug. 1984.
2. *Webster's New Collegiate Dictionary* (Springfield, Mass.: G. & C. Merriam, 1977).
3. Thomas J. Peters and Robert H. Waterman, Jr., *In Search of Excellence: Lessons from America's Best-Run Companies* (New York: Harper & Row, 1982).

Chapter 10
Managing Learning

1. Total Capacity required equals $1/(1 - R)$, where R is the fraction of product reworked during each cycle.

Chapter 12
Preventing Productivity Problems: Manufacturing
Line Architecture

1. *American Heritage Dictionary, New College Edition of the English Language* (Boston, Mass.: Houghton Mifflin, 1981).

Index

About the Authors

Bernard N. Slade was born in Sioux City, Iowa. He received a B.S.E.E. degree from the University of Wisconsin and an M.S. degree from Stevens Institute of Technology. He is now a consultant to the international consulting firm, Arthur D. Little, Inc., in Cambridge, Massachusetts. A pioneer in the early development of the semiconductor industry, his career has spanned thirty-six years in research, development, and manufacturing, including the position of Director of Manufacturing Technology with the IBM Corporation. He holds several patents and has published widely in the semiconductor field. He has also lectured to the Conference Board and has been a guest lecturer at several graduate schools of business and engineering, including Harvard and Stanford.

Raj Mohindra was born in Simla, India. He has a B. Tech. in mechanical engineering from the Indian Institute of Technology, Kanpur, and an M.S. in industrial engineering from The Ohio State University. He is head of the Productivity Competence Center at IBM where he has spent most of his twenty years in industry. He is a frequent guest lecturer at several of the leading graduate business schools, including Harvard and Stanford.